Life and Works
of Saint Sergius of Radonezh

Serge Jumati

Gozalov Books
The Hague

This book has the blessing of
His Eminence Simon, Archbishop of Brussels and Belgium and
temporarily of The Hague and the Netherlands

ISBN: 9789079889693; 978-90-79889-69-3

Editor: Convent of the Mother of God Portaitissa, Trazegnies, Belgium, portaitissa@skynet.be
Translators: Guram Kochi and Oxana Podyablonskaya
Illustrations: watercolor paintings by Natali Komarovskaya
Proefreading: Marijcke Tooneman and Wilfred Rosdorff
Design: Guram Kochi and Marijcke Tooneman
Cover image: a photo of an icon of Saint Sergius of Radonezh from the domestic chapel of the former Dutch Queen Anna Paulowna

© Gozalov Books, The Hague, 2022
Tel.: +31-70-352 15 65
E-mail: gozalovbooks@planet.nl
Website: www.hetsmallepad.nl

CONTENTS

"You came closer to God than any of the earthly ones": such are the words of one of the prayers to Saint Sergius of Radonezh. Saint Sergius revived in Russia the ascetic monastic practices, established several monasteries and trained nearly a hundred monks – ascetics who in their turn founded many monasteries, which illuminated the East and the North of Russia. Saint Sergius was at the same time a wise adviser and inspirer of Russian dukes, assisting the formation of the Russian state under the rule of the Grand Duke Dimitri Donskoy of Moscow. Having received a special blessing from Saint Sergius, Grand Duke Dimitri Donskoy rose up bravely against the Tartar Khan Mamai and defeated him in the bloody Battle of Kulikov, initiating the liberation of Russia from the Tartar yoke.

The first hagiography of Saint Sergius was written by his disciple Epiphanius the Wise, twenty-six years after the blissful passage of Radonezh's ascetic. There are more than ten different hagiographies of the Saint at present. The hagiography written by Metropolitan Philaret of Moscow is considered to be the best one. However, it is very concise as it is intended for reading in church during the Services and it does not contain details that are precious to the awestruck admirer of the great God-pleaser.

This work is mainly the narration taken from two books: the first – "The Life and Works of our Holy God-bearing father Sergius, Hegumen of Radonezh, Miracle-worker of all Russia by priest-monk Nikon (Rozhdestvensky), (first published in 1892), the second – "Saint Sergius of Radonezh and the Trinity Lavra founded by him" by the academician E. Golubinsky (1909). The original texts have been abridged and put into modern language.

Serge Jumati
Saint-Petersburg, January 2009

"I witness with my conscience that Saint Sergius stands with his hands lifted up before the throne of God and prays for all. Oh, if you just knew the power of his prayers and his love for us, you would have appealed to him every hour asking for help, protection and blessing for those, whom your heart aches for, relatives and beloved, both living here on earth and having passed into the eternal life."
Elder Zachariah, Schema-archimandrite of the Trinity Lavra of St. Sergius

Saint Sergius (secular name Bartholomew) was born in a family belonging to the nobility. The year of his birth has remained unknown. In some hagiographies it is stated as 1314, in others as 1322. The date of birth of the future ascetic was calculated as follows by the priest-monk Nikon: the commemoration day of the Apostle Bartholomew, whose name was given to the baby, is celebrated on the 11th June. The day when he was baptized, had to be, according to the tradition, the 40th day after his birth. Therefore, God's servant was born on the 3rd May. It is known that his father Cyril was a liege-man of the Rostov appanage dukes and was a member of a select circle of nobility. His mother's name was Maria. Bartholomew had two brothers: Stephen, the eldest and Peter, the youngest one. Bartholomew was born on an estate situated not more than four kilometres from Rostov-the-Great, on the way to Yaroslavl, not far from the Varnitsky Monastery of the Holy Trinity. Even before Bartholomew's birth, it was miraculously proclaimed that he would become a great servant of God. His mother, when still carrying him in her womb, went to church to attend the Sunday Liturgy. During the Liturgy, to the great amazement of all present, the baby in the womb screamed loudly three times: before the Gospel was read, before the Hymn of the Cherubim and when the priest spoke: "Let us be attentive! The Holy of the Holies!"

Epiphanius the Wise reminds us of the ancient saints who shone forth in the Old and the New Testament: both conception and birth of many of them were foretold by a peculiar revelation of God. Thus God had chosen and sanctified the prophet Jeremiah when he was still in the womb; another prophet, Isaiah, testifies the same about himself; and the holy and great Prophet and Christ's Baptist John being in the womb beheld God borne in the womb of the Blessed Virgin Mary; and the baby jumped up joyfully in the womb of his mother Elisabeth and through her mouth he cried out prophetically: "And whence is this to me, that the mother of my Lord should come to me?" (Lk. 1: 43). The parents of the holy prophet Elijah saw some light men swaddling the baby with fiery swaddling clothes and feeding him with a fiery flame.

"Like a miracle," Epiphanius continues, "was the cry of this baby in the womb of his mother; like a miracle was also the whole life of this truly miraculous man! God had marked him before the birth with His grace and with an unusual event He had indicated His especial Divine plan with regard to this baby".

It is told further in the book of Epiphanius the Wise that God also marked Bartholomew with a sign during his infancy. Bartholomew's family had noticed that he did not take the breast if his mother ate meat, and he always refused to take milk of wet-nurses. Thus Epiphanius the Wise explains this last peculiarity of the baby's behaviour: "The shoot from a good root had to be nourished with pure milk only." On Wednesdays and Fridays the baby did not want to take the breast at all. Hieromonk Nikon writes: "And this was repeated not once nor twice, but constantly; of course his mother worried about it, thought that the baby was unwell, asked advice of other women who examined the baby, but didn't find any symptom, neither of internal nor external disease, on the contrary, the baby not only did not cry but looked cheerfully at them, smiled and played with their hands." In this child's fasting "there were marked preceding inclinations of his mother and the seeds of his future inclinations became apparent", explains Metropolitan Philaret. "He was growing in the womb of his mother while she was fasting and after his birth it seemed that the baby was demanding her to fast. And she began indeed to observe fasting even more strictly: she ceased eating meat and the baby always took the breast after that, except on Wednesdays and Fridays."

When Bartholomew reached the age of seven his parents invited a tutor to teach their son reading and writing. In those times only children of nobles or prosperous people – dukes, boyars and merchants were educated. Reading and writing was taught strictly in the church spirit, using hagiographies and the Psalter. Unlike his brothers Bartholomew was not of a turn for studying at all and he was not able to write or read properly. His parents remonstrated with him, his tutor punished him, and his brothers laughed at him. But all of this was as Epiphanius the Wise tells, God's will that the child would receive the understanding of the Script not from people but from God. Bartholomew always pleaded with God in his prayer to give him the ability to understand reading and writing, to enlighten him and to make him understand. One day his father sent Bartholomew to find foals which were lost. In the field, he saw near an oak tree an old monk praying. The appearance of that monk struck him so much that he even forgot about his father's order. Having come nearer to the tree, Bartholomew waited for the monk to finish his prayer. Pious parents taught their children to invite travelling monks and pilgrims to their home, and Bartholomew wanted to invite him to share supper with them. When the elder finished his prayer he blessed the youth with the sign of the cross and asked him who he was, and where he was from. Bartholomew said his name and because of his naivety and warm disposition towards the elder, he told him, weeping, about his inability to learn reading and writing. The elder prayed to God for the enlightenment of the youth. Bartholomew prayed fervently together with him. At the end of the prayer the elder took out of his bag a small casket. He opened it, took small part of the holy prosphora, blessed the youth and said: "Take it, child and eat; it is given to you as the sign of God's grace and your understanding of the Holy Scripture. Mind not that the particle of the holy bread is so small: the pleasure of eating it is great. And do not bewail your current inability to read and write, for see, God will give you a greater understanding of books than your brothers and friends have, so that you will teach the others".

Then Bartholomew invited the elder to have a meal. The elder helped him to find the foals and together they went to the manor-house. When the elder met the parents of the youth, he, as usual, suggested to pray before the meal and asked him to read some psalms. Bartholomew said: "I cannot, Father." At this the elder said: "Henceforth the Lord grants you the ability of reading and writing." And the youth began to read well and clearly, to the great surprise of his parents.

After the meal, talking with Cyril and Maria, the elder said that the Lord had given them a blessed child. "You should know that your son will be great before God and men, because of his life, full of virtues!" The hospitable hosts went to see the elder to the gates, but when they came out of the house, the elder suddenly became invisible, and they assumed that it was an angel of God.

Meanwhile, the words of the elder were fulfilled: the youth read the Psalter and other books without difficulty, clearly understanding and explaining their meaning. Thus the gift of God, which was sent to him so unexpectedly, enlightened the mind of the young Bartholomew. Moreover, soon he surpassed in learning his brothers and comrades.

Since then Bartholomew's whole life was dedicated to God. He never missed a church service, read and reread the hagiographies, the writings of the holy Fathers, and chronicles. He spent his days in fasting and prayer, and wanted only one thing: to devote his life to God.

At the time when he became a young man Bartholomew's parents had lost nearly all their property. Their position at the Dukes of Rostov's court wavered. Bartholomew was born in the hard and dark period of Tartar domination over Russia. Priest-monk Nikon gives the following description of this epoch, taken from the book by the Russian historian Nicolas Karamzin: "An ancient Russian proverb: "close to the king – close to death" came into being when our Fatherland bore the chains of the Mongol yoke. Visiting the Horde was for the Russian dukes like attending the Final Judgement: happy was he who could return with the Khan's favour or at least, still having his head on his shoulders! Not seldom they even sacrificed their lives for the sake of the Christian faith and Holy Russia. That is why, departing for the Horde, they often wrote their last will, bidding a final farewell to their families. People were suffering because of the wilfulness of the rude and haughty Tartar tax-collectors, who went about all the towns and settlements. They had mercy for no one: they did everything that came into their heads: they robbed and set towns and villages on fire, they ruined and desecrated churches and killed or enslaved people. Even a petty Mongol merchant, even a Mongol tramp treated our ancestors as despicable slaves. Under such afflictions, with the lack of a centralized energetic administration, there was total freedom for mean people's passions, which are always present in abundance, but during such dark periods in history their amount increases spectacularly. The Tartar yoke influenced strongly social morality. "Having forgotten the national pride," Karamzin writes, "we learnt the mean cunning of slaves, which is the substitute of strength of the weak; deceiving the Tartars, we deceived each other even more badly; paying off barbarian violence, we became greedier and more insensible to offences, to shame, to the impudence of foreign tyrants.

 From the times of Basil Yaroslavich to the times of Ivan Kalita (the unhappiest period!) our Fatherland resembled more a dark forest than a state: power seemed to be the only justice; everybody who could rob actually did it, and not only strangers, but also their own kind; neither at home nor on the road could one feel safe; stealing became the ulcer of the common property."

In these times a modest appanage princedom in Moscow, of which Ivan Kalita was the duke began to grow stronger. Kalita was guided by the Metropolitan Peter. Priest-monk Nikon writes: "Shortly before his death Metropolitan Peter encouraged the duke by predicting the future greatness of Moscow's might. " If you, my son," he prophesied, "will honour my old age and will erect a church here, which will be worthy of the Mother of God, you will become more glorious than all the other princes, and your descendants will be extolled, my bones will remain in this city and the bishops will strive to dwell in it." Ivan Kalita fulfilled the behest of the elder-Metropolitan, and God blessed him by the success of his undertaking for the benefit of the Fatherland. Little by little Moscow began to reign over other cities, and Grand Duke Ivan merited the glorious name of unifier of the Russian lands. In a hundred years time nobody dared to question the first place of Moscow anymore: it united all the parts of Russia, and this consolidation not only had saved Russia from total devastation, but also had helped it to throw off the Mongolian yoke.

However this process of unifying many princedoms which had adapted themselves to the Tartar yoke and protected only their local interests and privileges, entailed violence: the power and the property of the appanage dukes and their vassals had been passed to the Moscow Duke and his vassals. In this way Bartholomew's parents had lost their manor and sought refuge in the small town of Radonezh, where Andrew, the juvenile son of Grand Duke Ivan Kalita, ruled. Stephen and Peter, Bartholomew's brothers, were already married and had entered the service of the- duke. Bartholomew in his turn continued in Radonezh his ascetic and prayerful life.

Thinking about the vanity of all earthly things, the blissful youth repeated often to himself the words of the prophet: "What profit is there in my blood, when I go down to the pit? (Ps. 30:9) . It is true that the world and everything that is in the world is created by God for the benefit of man, but all of this is perverted so much by human passions, violence and lies that the life of humans is nothing but toiling and illnesses, and he who wishes to work for the salvation of his soul, preserving for this the gentleness of spirit, meets obstacles and temptations from everywhere".

"O Lord!" thus he appealed during night vigils in heartfelt tenderness, "if what my parents told me is right, if even before my birth Thou hast already favoured to show on me, the wretched one, the marvellous signs of Thy divine grace, then let Thy will be done, Lord! Let Thy mercy, Lord, be with me! And let me, Lord, love Thee from my youth on with my whole heart and my whole soul and serve Thee alone, as I am committed to Thee from the womb of my mother; from the bosom of my mother Thou art my God! And as Thy mercy called on me, when I was yet in the womb of my mother, so don't forsake me now, Lord! My father and mother will abandon me when their time will come, but accept Thou me, make me Thine, reckon me among Thy chosen flock! I, the poor one, have been promised to Thee, from my birth; save me, Lord, from any impurity, from any filth of the soul and of the body, help me to consecrate myself in fear of Thee, Lord! Let my heart aspire to Thee only, don't let all the delights of this world soften me, don't let all the everyday amenities entice me; let my soul stick to Thee alone, and let Your right hand accept me... Don't permit me to ever rejoice with the joy of this world, but fill me, Lord, with spiritual joy and with the unspeakable Divine delight; thy spirit is good; lead me into the land of uprightness! (Ps. 143:10)"

Reasoning and praying in that way Bartholomew finally asked his parents to give him the blessing to follow the monastic way of life. His parents consented to bless him, but they asked him first to take care of them in their old age and to enter the monastery after their death. Bartholomew, being a loving son, remained with his parents. However his aspiration for the monastic life was so strong that his parents little by little came to think the same way and went to the Pokrovsky Khotkov monastery, not far from Radonezh.

In olden times there existed such monasteries with separate housing for old men and women.

Russia was at that time like a kind of network of small principalities in which towns and settlements were arising and growing rapidly. The town monasteries and those on the outskirts were founded because of the zeal of the high Orthodox clergy, or on behest of dukes, boyars, rich townsfolk. Each newly installed duke endeavoured to adorn his principality with a cloister. Any town, especially one with a duke's court, was not considered to be well-equipped if there were no monastery or cathedral in it. Such monasteries, being situated amidst the worldly life, in daily contact with it also for its religious needs, were called "worldly cloisters". It is quite probable that this was not a monastery in the full meaning of this word, but a parish church, which gave shelter to old men and women.

According to the Russian historian V.O. Klyuchevsky "for the inhabitants there was a place where in their old age, they could take the monastic vows and take care of the future life of their souls in the other world." This place gave shelter to pious members of the gentry and to helpless people of the peasant communities: lonely people, cripples, old maids whom no one wanted to marry, and beggars. Their cells in the Khotkov monastery were situated next to the Pokrovsky church. All the people living in the monastery, monks, nuns, old men and women, beggars were engaged in various crafts and regularly organized public sales, which were visited by the inhabitants of Khotkovo. Thereby it was the custom that public sales and trade fairs were held not outside the walls of the cloister, but inside it.

In that very monastery the elder brother of Bartholomew, Stephen had taken monastic vows some years earlier after the sudden death of his wife.

Having lived in the cloister for a short period of time Cyril and Maria passed away. Having buried his parents and given his entire heritage to his younger brother Peter who also took upon himself to care for the children of Stephen, Bartholomew began to fulfil his dearest wish.

Specific for the cloisters in the XIVth century, was that they observed the Greek rule of monastic life, which did not necessarily impose to live in seclusion. However, the rule of life of the ancient Egyptian founders of monasticism, the venerable Anthony, Pachomius and Macarius, who had been engaged in ascetic practices in remote seclusion in the desert, was closer to the heart of the young ascetic, and he decided to follow in their footsteps.

It might have been too hard or even impossible for the young and inexperienced Bartholomew to follow this way of life alone. For besides spiritual temptations he had to beware of wild beasts and wicked people. Bartholomew implored his elder brother to live in the desert together with him. Stephen was not so eager to commit himself to such a heavy undertaking. He had taken monastic vows in the Khotkov monastery, not because he had an elevated goal to serve God but in order to heal his broken heart and the wounds of his soul. He did have spiritual aspirations, but at the same time, a strong attachment to the secular life; therefore he did not want to be a hermit. But persistently and purposefully, Bartholomew was able to persuade his brother. With a little property and some tools they started the search for an appropriate place. Twelve kilometres from Khotkovo the brothers saw a place that took their fancy right away. It was a small hill with its top rising above the neighbourhood; therefore it was named Makovitsa (the crown on the head). It was surrounded on all sides by wild forest, still untouched by man. There was a spring, although at some distance from the top. The brothers stood praying. Placing themselves in God's hands they asked Him to bless their labour and abiding.

In the beginning the hermits built themselves a cabin from branches and then they began to chop wood to build their cells and the

church. Working with their hands was for them an obligatory part
of the ascetic life.

Hermit Bartholomew

When the church was ready for consecration, Bartholomew said to Stephen:

"You are my elder brother in the flesh and in spirit you are a father to me. So tell me, in the name of which saint should our church be consecrated?"

"Why do you ask me something you know better than I do?" answered the elder brother. "You remember certainly our parents told you more than once in my presence: "Watch over yourself, child: you are already not ours, but God's; God has chosen you before your birth and given about you a good sign, when you cried three times in your mother's womb during the liturgy." And the priest who baptised you and the miraculous elder who visited us, said then that this thrice-repeated cry had presaged that you will be a disciple of the most Holy Trinity; so let our church be devoted to the most holy Name of the Life-giving Trinity. Thus it would be not according to our will, but according to God's will: let His Name be blessed here from now on and unto the ages of ages!"

Bartholomew and Stephen went on foot to Moscow to ask Metropolitan Theognost's blessing for the consecration of the church. The Metropolitan received the petitioners favourably and sent with them a priest, who took a holy antimension with the relics of holy martyrs, and everything required for the consecration of the church. On request of the brothers, the church was consecrated in the name of the Holy and Life-Giving Trinity. Thus, modestly and in a spirit of eremitical humility, the foundation was laid of the Lavra of the Holy Trinity, which was many times glorified by Saint Sergius' deeds. Priest-monk Nikon, the composer of the hagiography of this great Saint, refers the foundation to the year 1340. "Rightly this church," remarks blessed Epiphanius the Wise, "was consecrated in the name of the Holy Trinity: it was founded by the Grace of God the Father, by the mercy of the Son and with the help of the Holy Spirit." The brothers passed their days in fasting and prayer, in labour and patience. For Bartholomew, their secluded life was a joy: he became dead to the world, and the world was dead to him, and he could dedicate himself fully to the service of God. For Stephen however, it all was just toiling and deprivation. He was probably not ready, not only for the exploits of living in seclusion, but even for the monastic life. Stephen retired to the Khotkov cloister in search of a peaceful haven after the death of his beloved wife. In the dense forest, with the rough circumstances of the hermit's life, the spirit of despondency took hold of him. No matter how hard Bartholomew tried to persuade him to struggle with this temptation, to endure afflictions, Stephen did not listen to him and retired to Moscow's Bogoyavlensky cloister. He made his monastic cell more comfortable and began a monastic way of life which was more suitable for him. God determines a specific path for everybody and does not ask us to carry a load above our strength. Stephen came to love the monastic life, worked hard and lived a strict life.

At that time the future Metropolitan Alexis of All Russia had been working as an ordinary monk at the same Bogoyavlensky Monastery. Stephen and Alexis were kindred spirits; they stood side by side in the church and sang together in the church choir. Their mentor and adviser was a skilled elder, called Gerontius. Metropolitan Theognost was benevolent to Stephen, Gerontius and Alexis, and invited them from time to time for conversations on spiritual matters. The Grand Duke Simeon Ivanovich, the son of Ivan Kalita, also paid special attention to Stephen and Alexis. At his request metropolitan Theognost ordained Stephen to the priesthood and appointed him hegumen of the Bogoyavlensky Monastery. Then the Grand Duke chose Stephen as his confessor. Basil, a capital's captain of a thousand soldiers, his brother Theodore and other noble boyars followed the example of the duke.

Young Bartholomew in his turn had been training himself to endure all the works and exploits not only of physical but also of the spiritual kind. Only when he found that he had tested himself sufficiently, he began zealously asking God to vouchsafe him with the angelic image, i.e. the monastic rank.

In one of the monasteries near Radonezh there was an elder, the humble hegumen Metrophanes. Bartholomew grew spiritually close to him, maybe even before his retiring into seclusion. Also hegumen Metrophanes might have visited the hermit in his solitude and celebrated the Divine Liturgy in the new church. Blessed Epiphanius tells us nothing about it but he mentions that Bartholomew had asked hegumen Metrophanes to visit him in his hermitage, and had been ineffably pleased with his visit. Bartholomew had received the hegumen as a welcome heaven sent guest and had assiduously asked him to stay some time in his cell. The kind elder had willingly agreed.

After a little time, the blessed youth asked the elder to admit him to the monastic rank. "Father", Bartholomew said, "commit the deed of love for the sake of God; and make me a monk, for I came to love this rank from my youth on and I have wished to become a monk for a long time. Only the will of my parents kept me from this, but now, God be praised, I am free from all and as a deer thirsts for water springs, I thirst with heart and soul for the monastic secluded life."

The hegumen returned to his monastery, invited some monks and having gathered everything necessary for a monastic consecration, he went back to the hermit. On the 7th October 1342 the twenty three-year-old youth took his monastic vows in the small and poorly decorated hermit's church. On this day the Holy Church celebrates the memory of the Holy Martyrs Sergius and Bacchus. As it was the custom of the church, Bartholomew was named Sergius.

Having accomplished the ceremony of consecration, Hegumen Metrophanes celebrated Divine Liturgy and administered the Sacrament to the monk. The newly admitted monk was filled with the grace of the Holy Spirit and there was a breath of ineffable fragrance in the church and this marvellous fragrance was spread even beyond the temple. The eye-witnesses of this miracle told this later, glorifying God who reveals His servants.

The young monk spent seven days in the church without leaving it. Every day the hegumen celebrated the Divine Liturgy and administered the Sacrament to him. On all these days Sergius ate nothing but prosphoras. Psalms and chants were constantly on his lips. Comforting himself with them he praised God and appealed to Him from the bottom of his grateful heart: "Lord, I have loved the habitation of Thy house, and the place where Thine honour dwelleth. (Ps. 26, 8). Thy testimonies are very sure: holiness becometh Thine house, O Lord, for ever. (Ps. 93, 5). How amiable are Thy tabernacles, O Lord of hosts!

My soul longeth, yea, even fainteth for the courts of the Lord: my heart and my flesh crieth out for the living God. Yea, the sparrow (my soul) hath found an house, and the swallow a nest for herself, where she may lay her young, even Thine altars, O Lord of hosts, my King, and my God. Blessed are they that dwell in Thy house: they will be still praising Thee. Selah.

Blessed is the man whose strength is in Thee; in whose heart are the ways of them. (Ps. 84, 1–5). For a day in Thy courts is better than a thousand. I had rather be a doorkeeper in the house of my God, than to dwell in the tents of wickedness. (Ps. 84, 11)"

In this way his soul rejoiced and burned with the divine fire!

Seven days passed as one day, and the time had come for Sergius to part with the elder- hegumen.

"Father," the young monk said to the elder with gentle melancholy, "you leave me alone in this uninhabited desert... I have been wishing for a long time to seclude myself and always asked God for it, remembering the words of the Prophet: I wander far off, and remain in the wilderness. (Ps. 55:7) And blessed be God, Who did not leave my prayer fruitless; I thank His kindness that He did not deprive me of this mercy: to live in seclusion and keep silence... You go away, Father, bless me, the humble one, and pray that my solitude may remain unbroken... Make me understand how a monk should live alone, how to pray to God, how to avoid harm for the soul, how to oppose the enemy and the thoughts of pride... I am still a beginner-monk; I must ask your advice in all things!"

The elder wondered at the humility of mind of the newly tonsured one.

"Why do you question me, a sinner, about the things that you know yourself no less than I do, o, praiseworthy head!", Metrophanes said. "You have trained yourself to fulfil every spiritual exploit; it leaves me only to wish that God Himself will make you understand and will lead you to perfection."

The elder then had a little talk with Sergius about different cases in the spiritual practices and left. At parting, the monk Sergius threw himself at his feet and asked once more for his blessing and prayers. "Pray, pray, Father," he said, "that God would give me strength to withstand fleshly warfare and demonic temptations, that He would guard me against fierce beasts amidst my eremitical works."

"Blessed be God," the elder said to him and a strong faith sounded in his words, "He does not allow temptations to come upon us which are too strong for us to withstand; the Apostle speaks to comfort us: "I can do all this through the Lord Jesus Who gives me strength." (Phil. 4:13) Going away I commend you to God's care; God will be your refuge and strength. He will help you to withstand the crafty designs of the enemy. God loves those who are well-pleasing for Him, He will protect you here and in eternity."

In conclusion hegumen Metrophanes said to monk Sergius that God would establish a great and famous monastery on the place of his hermitage. Then he said a short prayer, blessed the monk and departed.

The hermit stayed alone in his dearly loved solitude, without elder and brother, without mentor and helper, alone with God the Omnipresent, He who never forsakes those who have left everything behind for His sake.

For the reader to be able to imagine the heaviness of Saint Sergius' anchoretic exploit, we shall outline its difficulties, as they have been described by people who have followed this narrow and hard path. The hermit begins his way joyfully: nobody forced him; a passionate zeal for asceticism enticed him to the life in seclusion. All sorrows and privations seem a delight to him, his prayer finds its expression in tears, and he entirely burns with the fire of divine desire... But see: the first delight passes. Days of dryness of the soul follow, an excruciating anguish seizes him, his thoughts don't obey his reason, and the soul is eager to escape the cross and becomes cold towards anything that is spiritual. And above all there are hunger, thirst, cold and danger from the attacks of wild animals. Meanwhile, the world entices the hermit by the memories of the past, where it was warm and comfortable. Why shouldn't he return to the cloister, where the kind brethren would share his sorrows, help to struggle against the enemies with wise advice and brotherly prayer? Thus the world and the flesh bother the hermit with their demands, not to mention the sinful impulses of the heart, when gusts of passion rise like a tempest and drive the hermit back into the world, burning him from within. And if it were not for God's Grace which comforts the hermit by touching his suffering heart, if it were not for the power of Christ which realises itself through weakness, no hermit could withstand this excruciating and back-breaking struggle. But these are not all the difficulties of living in solitude. Even when God-sent consolations stream into the hermit's soul, tempting thoughts of pride at his achievements, that sometimes drive careless hermits into a moral lapse or insanity, try to penetrate into his heart. Thereby the zealot of the spiritual life struggles in proportion to his success not against blood and flesh, but against evil spirits from the underworld. "As soon," the holy hierarch Philaret says, "as these invisible enemies notice that a man has left the world behind and renounced the flesh trying to penetrate further and further into the spiritual sphere to be closer to the heavenly Powers and God himself, then, to impede him, they not only rush towards him with incredible impudence and shoot at him with burning arrows of evil intentions from afar, but they also intrude into his imagination and feelings and show him odd images and hallucinations". Sometimes these visions aim at fascinating the hermit with the false idea that he is already holy: in this case he should protect himself on all sides. As early as his childhood Saint Sergius trained himself to struggle with the flesh, its passions and sinful desires. Elevating his spirit by thinking of God, he also strengthened his body by constant work. In winter when the ground was cracked by the hard frost, he, like a bodiless one, without warm clothes, enduring severe cold, would think only of how to avoid the everlasting fire. "Never in his life did he complain or grumble about anything, he was never depressed and he never grieved. Never! He was always satisfied with eve-rything, even when in need, he never worried, even about man's temptation and sorrow", the holy hierarch Platon writes. Indeed Saint Sergius could boldly repeat the Apostle's words: "the world is crucified unto me, and I unto the world (Gal 6:14)"; owing to God's Grace I live as if I didn't have anything to do with the secular world." He was the true warrior of Christ God invested with God's weapons against all the weaknesses of humanity and devilish temptations. Sergius destroyed the fears and delusions of life in solitude like a thin cobweb. And the Lord protected him with His grace and Ser-gius saw God's protecting Hand on himself and glorified Him day and night.

Father Sergius himself once told his disciples that one night he had come to the church for Matins, and as soon as he had started his prayer the church wall broke in two before him and Satan entered through this opening, like a thief who doesn't use doors. He was accompanied by a whole devilish regiment – they all were wearing pointed hats and Lithuanian clothes, who in those times scared the Russians no less than Tartars. The pretended Lithuanians rushed to ruin the church with noise and savage yells gnashing their teeth in anger, their blasphemous jaws belching fire.

"Go away," they yelled at the hermit. "Don't you dare stay here any longer, we didn't attack you, but you attacked us! If you stay here, we will tear you to pieces, and you will die at our hands."

"The devil has this habit," writes blessed Epiphanius, probably repeating a didactic remark of his great teacher, "this powerless enemy has this habit: he boasts with pride and threatens that he will shake the ground and dry up the sea, though he himself, as a fallen spirit, doesn't have power even over a herd of pigs. (See Mt 8:31, 32)"

Saint Sergius wasn't confused by these powerless threats and his prayer to God became stronger.

"Many, O Lord my God, are Thy wonderful works which Thou hast done (Ps. 40:5)", he used the words of the Psalmist, "Keep not Thou silence, O God: hold not Thy peace, and be not still, O God. For, lo, Thine enemies make a tumult: and they that hate Thee have lifted up their head. (Ps. 83:1-2) Let God arise, let His enemies be scattered: let them also that hate Him flee before Him. As smoke is driven away, so drive them away: as wax melteth before the fire, so let the wicked perish at the presence of God. (Ps. 67:1-2)" The fallen spirits couldn't stand the fire of the prayer and disappeared as suddenly as they emerged.

Another time the whole monastic cell of the hermit became full of abominable snakes so that the floor couldn't even be seen. Once when he was reading the night rule in his hut, a noise suddenly swept past the woods and all around his cell demonic yells could be heard: "Get away from here! Why did you come to the thick of the forest, what do you want to find here? Don't hope to live here longer than another hour, you see, this place is deserted and impassable, aren't you afraid to starve to death here or be killed by murderers? And then somebody will find your corpse and say: "This was a useless man!" Wild animals are walking around you in the desert, they are waiting to tear you to pieces and we are not going to leave you alone, we will not let you live in this place, empty from time immemorial. So if you don't want to die suddenly, run away from here right now not looking back or around, or you will find death at our hands!"

And again the hermit turned to God in tearful prayer, and again God's power strengthened him and the demons disappeared. The hermit's heart overflowed with spiritual delight and he realized that from now on he was forever given the victorious power to tread on serpents and scorpions, and over all the power of the enemy (Luke 10:19); and he glorified and praised God in gratitude, rejoicing in spirit like a new Moses, with the words from Holy Scripture: "I thank you, O my Lord," he appealed from the depth of his grateful heart, "Thou hast not abandoned me, but heard me promptly and forgave me! Thou hast shown me a token for good; that they which hate me may see it, and be ashamed: because thou, Lord, hast holpen me, and comforted me. (Ps. 86:17) Thy right hand, O Lord, is become glorious in power: Thy right hand, O Lord, hath dashed in pieces the enemy. (Exodus 6:15)"

From these stories about the holy God-pleaser, which have been noted down by his disciple, can be seen the bitter persistence, with which the gloomy army of the spirit of darkness took up their arms against the hermit at the beginning of his spiritual practices. Saint Epiphanius remarks that "the enemy was afraid that in this deserted place a sacred dwelling of monks would appear to glorify God's name and to save many souls; he wanted to drive away Saint Sergius, envying his and our salvation". So, Satan or as Saint Barsanuphius the Great calls him, "the perfidious elder", having a thousand years experience of struggling with Christian hermits, saw how strong this man of prayer was to deal with. That's why he aimed all his efforts to stop the hermit at the beginning of his exploit because later it would no longer be possible. What do all the intrigues of Satan mean in comparison with Christ's grace? What are all the efforts of the powerless enemy, despite all his anger, in comparison with God the Almighty? We all know that Saint Sergius won this struggle and founded the Monastery of Radonezh, which became the main monastery of all the cloisters in deserts and cities of the wide Russian territory.

We have already said that demons often appeared to the hermit in the shape of wild animals and beasts which wanted to tear him to pieces. After such visions the fear of real wild animals was "the least fear" to him. Packs of wolves scoured the woods around his hut; their eyes were sparkling ominously in the darkness. Sometimes other even more terrible inhabitants of deserted forests, namely bears, appeared there. Because of human infirmity, an unintentional fear would seize his heart for a moment at the thought of his helpless loneliness, but then he would immediately protect himself with prayer, and this fear would be transmitted to the animals who ran away to the forest, having done him no harm.

One day God's servant saw in front of his hut a big bear and as he understood that the bear was not so much fierce as hungry, the hermit took pity on him and put a piece of bread on a stub. The animal liked this treat so much that he started visiting the hermit's hut, waiting for his piece of bread and staring at the hermit with a sort of kind expression in his eyes. Sometimes the guest from the forest stayed longer looking around like "a wicked lender who wants insistently to have his debt back". Saint Sergius thanked God for sending him the ferocious beast as a kind of consolation, and remembering the words from Holy Scripture: "A righteous man regardeth the life of his beast. (Proverbs 12:9-11)" got accustomed to feeding the beast. The hermit shared the last piece of bread with it, and sometimes even gave it the whole meal, because the bear didn't observe the fast. The hermit didn't have any other food than bread in his cell, and sometimes there wasn't even any bread left. It was probably his brother Peter, who lived in Radonezh, who brought him bread from time to time.

Thus the God-pleaser trained himself to renounce even the most essential necessities. "Maybe," the holy hierarch Philaret says, "in this peaceful treatment of fierce beasts he contemplated the evidence

of the original obedience of all animals to the innocent human be-
ings." That is why the beasts obeyed his word and became tame like
sheep.

Saint Sergius had served God diligently in his solitude – the time
had now come to serve his neighbour for the sake of God. He listened to God's will and didn't renounce another's burden according
to the word of the Apostle: "Bear ye one another's burdens, and so
fulfil the law of Christ. (Gal 6:2); Look not every man on his own
things, but every man also on the things of others. (Phil 2:4)"

Chapter 4. The Hegumen

"A city that is set on a hill cannot be hid." (Matthew. 5:14). A fragrant flower cannot be hidden even amidst the wild grass: it will be found by its perfume; so also Saint Sergius couldn't hide himself in the wild forest. The fragrance of his holy life spread far, and people who had a purified spiritual sense or those who desired such purification felt this fragrance with their hearts. The sorrowful circumstances of that time disposed people even more to run away from civilization to deserted woods. Thank God there was a man full of Divine grace, who was able to slake the soul's thirst, to kindle and to keep a light in it, and with the warmth of which it is easier to bear the load of life and the good Christ's yoke.

Not more than two or three years had passed since the hermit had secluded himself in the thick of the forest, when in Radonezh and in the near settlements people started to talk about the young anchorite. "Some," as Pachomius Logofet writes, "would speak about his strict abstention, hard work and other exploits; others would wonder at his simplicity and mildness; some other would tell about his power over evil spirits, some would revere his resignation and purity of the soul." So, one by one people started coming to him, at first for conversation, useful for the soul, and for spiritual advice, and later people appeared who wanted to live near him. Sometimes groups of two or three men came at the same time and prostrated themselves before him, imploring him to let them settle nearby.

It grieved the hermit to give up his solitude. Also he worried that the severe desert might disappoint brothers, who might leave this place grumbling, as those cowardly disciples of Christ who said: "This is an hard saying; who can bear it? (Jn 6:60)"

At first Saint Sergius didn't let them live there, telling them about the difficulties of a life in solitude.

"Could you bear the barrenness of this place?" he used to say. "You will struggle here with hunger, thirst and other privations."

"We are prepared to bear anything, praiseworthy Father," they would answer, "and we will bear anything with the Lord's help through your holy prayers: just don't send us away, don't make us leave this blessed place."

Seeing their desire, strong faith in God's help and remembering the word of the Saviour: "and him that cometh to me I will in no wise cast out." (Jn. 6:37), the hermit decided to accept them.

"I wished, my brethren," he used to say, "to end my days in solitude, but because of your entreaties I remembered God's word: "For where two or three are gathered together in my name, there am I in the midst of them. (Mt. 18:20)." And David sings in his psalms: "Behold, how good and how pleasant it is for brethren to dwell together in unity! (Ps 133:1)"

That is why I, a sinful man, don't want to oppose God's will, Who wishes to create a monastery here. I accept you joyfully; each of you can build a monastic cell for himself, but you should know, that if you really came here for God's work and if you want to live here with me, so you should be prepared to bear any indigence and sorrow, for Scripture says: As you start working for God, prepare your soul for temptation (Sir.2:1); and "the kingdom of heaven suffereth violence." (Mt.11:12)

So they started to build their cells near the cell of monk Sergius and with a child's love they learned from him the spiritual practices of seclusion. The first one who came to the hermit was Basil, called the Dry, maybe because of his strict abstention. He came from the upper reaches of the Dubna river, and was already advanced in age, and after living with the teacher for a while he passed away to the Lord. The other disciple and co-worker of Sergius was a farmer named Jacob, whom the brethren called "Yakuta". His work of obedience was taking care of deliveries. However, as Saint Epiphanius tells us, Yakuta was sent outside the cloister only in case of extreme necessity and therefore not often. Two other disciples, who came with the first group, were the deacon Onesimus and Elisa, his son; they came originally from the same district as Sergius. Onesimus is mentioned among the inhabitants of Rostov, who moved to Radonezh at the same time as the pious parents of Bartholomew. Among the first disciples of the great hermit were also the future Saint, Silvestre Obnorsky, Methodius Peshnoshsky, Andronicus Moskovsky and some others, twelve in total.

When the brethren had built their twelve cells, Saint Sergius let them enclose the cells with a high wooden paling as a protection against wild animals, and he appointed Onesimus, whose dwelling was near the entrance, as a porter. Thick forest surrounded the cloister on all sides, the crowns of the old trees were rustling right above the cells. Stumps and logs were lying all over the yard and on the little space left free different vegetable crops were sowed to supply the hermits with meagre meals. So humble was Sergius' monastery in the first years of its existence!

The life of the hermits in the new cloister passed quietly. There was no hegumen, even no priest, but the order of the everyday services was strictly observed, except the Liturgy. The hermits' day began in the middle of the night, according to the words of the Psalmist: to praise God seven times a day (Ps 119:164). Every day the hermits went to the church for the midnight service, matins, third, sixth and ninth hour, vespers and compline, often singing prayers in between. There can be found in manuscripts preserved in monastic libraries from those times, canons for those who give alms, for the sick and for the dead. Unceasing prayer, according to the apostle's commandment, (1 Col 5:17), was their permanent rule in the church as well as in the cell. For the Liturgy on the days of the Church feasts, a priest from the nearest settlement or hegumen Mitrophan, who admitted Bartholomew to the monastic vows, would be invited. The accomplisher of God's mysteries was always received joyfully and with proper honour.

A year later, as the brethren lived together, hegumen Mitrophan joined Sergius' monastery. Sergius rejoiced, for he hoped that Mitrophan would become the head of the anchorites. Mitrophan indeed became the first permanent priest and Father Superior of Sergius' cloister. However it did not last long, for soon he passed away. About twelve years had passed since the first co-anchorites joined Sergius in his solitude, but the new monks' dwelling still didn't have a Father Superior. Sergius didn't want to become hegumen or priest because of his humble wisdom. He governed the cloister by means of his own example only: he was following God's word, because he was the "servant of all". (Mk.9,35). He served the brethren, as blessed Epiphanius expressed it, "as a bought slave": he hewed and split wood, grinded grain in the hand millstone, baked bread, cut out and sewed clothes and shoes; he brought water from the spring and put the buckets near the cell of each brother. Unanimity and brotherly love reigned among the hermits. Such an "absence of a head" was in fact stronger than any order existing in the world. Just one word from their beloved teacher could stop any arguing and impel the monks to observe the monastic rules.

Sergius was a true leader of his disciples, however without ecclesiastical rank he could not be their spiritual Father in the sacrament of confession. He realised of course that the monastery needed a spiritual pastor and he prayed assiduously to God to send them a Father Superior. By that time however the brethren paid a visit to Sergius' cell asking him unanimously and resolutely to become their Father Superior. Sergius opposed their demand by referring to his unworthiness, but finally the disciples obtained his consent to visit the archbishop, who would resolve this matter. According to the evidence of the blessed Epiphanius, the bishop Athanasius Volynsky, who lived in Pereyaslavl-Zalessky and conducted the metropolitan's business, ordained monk Sergius to the priesthood and appointed him hegumen. Metropolitan Alexis of Moscow was not in Russia at that time as in 1354 he was on a journey to Constantinople for church affairs.

At first the cloister of Saint Sergius was a monastery where the monks lived separately, where they lived by a "hermitage rule". Each hermit had his own cell, located at some distance from the others. There he prayed, fasted, did some handiwork or other to earn his living. The brethren came together only for church prayers. Those were the monastic traditions of ancient Palestinian monasteries and some on Mount Athos. In the same way Sergius, when he started to accept people who wished to live near him, suggested to each of them to build their own personal cells. But every new hermit was probably not left alone, the brethren rendered him help. The great hermit was an assiduous assistant of all the brethren, as he was a good carpenter.

Sergius, as Father Superior, resembled Theodosius Pecherski: he used the same strictness towards himself and love for the brethren. He spent the same hardworking, sleepless nights, he exposed the idle; he held the same calm, meek speeches, with tears of fatherly love. He remained the same with regard to the brethren, even after acceding to the rank of hegumen: just as before he taught rather by his own example than by word. Every day he celebrated the Divine Liturgy, and neither tiredness, nor daily business and concerns would hamper him being the first at any service and the last to leave the church.

According to the monastery rules the brethren were not allowed to communicate or see each other after compline, except for special needs, when it was necessary for instance to talk to the hegumen. Father Sergius watched strictly that this rule was observed. Sometimes at night, after prayers, the solicitous hegumen silently went round all the cells. Through the small windows the elder could see what the brethren were doing. If a monk was praying or doing needlework, writing, reading a holy book or was deep in thoughts – the hegumen was glad, thanked God for him and prayed for the strengthening of a toiler in the exploit of salvation. But if he heard conversation he knocked on the door or window and went away. The next morning he would call the chatterers and would start a conversation about monastic responsibilities and without exposing them, speaking as if about others, he inclined them to a meek confession of their sins. A meek and obedient monk would confess it instantly, would ask and receive absolution from the hegumen, but sometimes, an unreasonable monk would evade confession. In this case the hegumen would expose him with meekness and love, according to the word of the Psalmist: "Let the righteous smite me; it shall be a kindness: and let him reprove me. (Ps 141:5)"; and if a monk still persisted, the hegumen would impose a penance on him. Thus the loving father held out a helping hand to his powerless sons; he could combine meekness with strictness, without indulging negligence and without giving occasion to despondency.

During a certain period the number of brethren in the cloister remained the same: twelve people, the hegumen was the thirteenth. New people came and replaced those who couldn't bear a solitary life and those who passed away; so the number stayed the same. It was this way until archimandrite Simon came from Smolensk, the first, who made up the number of the monks to thirteen. After his coming the number of monks in the cloister of Father Sergius began to grow further.

Archimandrite Simon, known for his virtues and strict life in Smolensk, had heard of Saint Sergius' deeds and left his rank, honour and respect in Smolensk, his native place, friends, relations and with the crook of an ordinary wanderer he came to Radonezh's hermitage. With deep humility he asked the hegumen to accept him, and Saint Sergius accepted the humble archimandrite with love and joy. Assiduously Simon spent many years in obedience to the holy hegumen. Thanks to his donation a new cathedral of the Trinity, also in wood, but more spacious was built. Adorned with all the virtues of a hermit, Simon passed away in old age and hegumen Sergius celebrated his burial service with great honour.

Sergius' cloister was slowly extending and looked on the outside as a quite prosperous dwelling. There, where before there was only an impenetrable forest where frightening bears had walked and not a trace of a human being could be found, now the cloister was flourishing. Monks' cells, at first built in the middle of the wild wood and placed without any order, now stood in a quadrilateral around the church, which appeared to be in the centre of the cloister in its modest beauty and could be seen from all the monastery cells. And in that cathedral and in those poor monastery cells, the eulogy to God sounded unceasingly. In the silence of the hermitage the humble monks were working diligently under the experienced leadership of hegumen Sergius for the purification of their hearts from passions, trying to forget that another world existed outside the hermitage, the world which is stirring noisily as a changeable sea, immersing people in the turbid waves of life's vanity...

"There is a story in the ancient Fathers' books," blessed Epiphanius remarks. "Once the holy Fathers came together and started talking about the end of times. In prophetic spirit they said that in the last times people will be weak and there will not be such great ascetics and zealots as there were among the first hermits. But see: God strengthened Saint Sergius and showed him in the last generation to be as one of the ancient fathers. He settled in the thick of the forest, having no fear of demonic delusions and for this God guarded his cloister by regiments of angels. Many people came to him to work for the salvation of their souls in his peaceful shelter, and he didn't reject anyone – neither old, nor young, nor rich nor poor: he accepted everyone with joy and love according to the words of the Gospel: "and him that cometh to me I will in no wise cast out. (Jn 6:37)", but he was not quick in allowing them to make their monastic vows. He would order to dress a newcomer in a long overall made of coarse black cloth and would assign him to do one or other work of penance with the other brethren, until he would be used to the monastic rules. Then he would give him "monastic clothes", or, as it is called nowadays, he would become a "ryasofor" (a novice, who is not yet admitted to the monastic vows) and only after thorough trials he would allow him to take his vows and give him the right to wear the klobuk. And when he noticed that the monk had become experienced in spiritual work, he would vouchsafe him the sacred schema".

The number of brethren increased little by little. "Virtue," says blessed Epiphanius, "exposes him who obtained it in the same way as a burning candle does with the one who is carrying it. As a spring attracts deer, so the Grace-giving gifts of Sergius' soul attracted those who sought salvation. "

The Apostle Paul, according to his own account, worked day and night with his hands in order not to live at anyone else's expense and not to be a burden to anybody, though as an evangelist of Salvation he had a full right hereto (see 1 Col. 2: 7–9). The holy ascetics and zealots of Christ strictly observed the same rule; also Father Sergius established it in his cloister. Each monk had to earn his daily bread by the labour of his hands, and in case of deficiency he had to ask and await with patience God's favour. So he taught by word and deed.

Father Sergius' cloister at that time was in every sense of the word a wilderness. "It was surrounded for many kilometres," tells blessed Epiphanius, "by dense, impenetrable forests abounding with all kinds of wild animals – from a timid hare to a blood-thirsty wolf and a terrible bear". Who would visit hermits and bring them some provisions in such backwoods? On the other hand, in those times there was no communal life established in Sergius' dwelling. Hermits met only for church Services, the rest of the day or the night everyone worked for himself, in his secluded cell: there were neither common meals, nor common works of obedience. It is no wonder that Father Sergius' monastery being rich with piety often was in need of the most elementary things. "Everything one needed was not there," blessed Epiphanius writes, "quite often the brethren had neither a piece of bread, nor a handful of flour or salt; not to mention oil or other seasonings. The hermits had to go through a lot of trials living in such a wilderness, but Father Sergius had a strong faith in God, that was tested by sorrows and God answered him according to his faith: he laid his hope in God and God never forsook him!"

Sometimes there wasn't enough wine for the liturgy, wheat for prosphoras, incense for censing and the hermits suffered want in the Divine Service; sometimes there was not enough wax for candles, oil for icon lamps – they would then light pieces of birch or pine which crackled and smoked while burning. And by such light they would hold morning or night services, hardly being able to read canons and Psalms in the semi-darkness. Such a service was no less pleasing to God than a ceremonial service conducted in the magnificent cathedrals by the light of countless icon lamps and numerous candles, for the hearts of the holy zealots shone more silently and brighter than any candle, and the fire of their prayers trembled with their lamentations, which from the depth of their hearts ascended to the throne of God!

According to the testimony of Saint Joseph of Volokolamsk there was such poverty in Saint Sergius' cloister, such unwillingness to gain that even books were sometimes written on birch bark because of the lack of money to purchase parchment. Their church utensils did not shine with gold. Nowadays pilgrims examine with awesome wonder in the Lavra's vestry the relics of the holy hermit: the wooden vessels used by Saint Sergius for the Divine Liturgy, and his simple raiment.

Hegumen Sergius cared for his daily bread least of all and quite often he was the first to suffer the lack of food. And he, who fasted since his infancy, endured privations with a grateful heart, giving an example to the brethren. The hegumen only permitted to accept what was brought to the cloister by pious peasants and he admonished the faint-hearted to put their trust in the Lord. This firm trust in God's favour never put him to shame.

Once he had neither bread nor salt and there was an extreme scarcity in the whole cloister. The humble hegumen spent three days without food and at dawn of the fourth day he took an axe and went to one of the brothers called Daniel.

"I heard, elder", he told the hermit, "that you wish to build an inner porch attached to your cell. Allow me to construct it for you so that my hands won't be idle."

"That's true," Daniel replied, "I would like very much to construct it. I have everything ready for this work since long ago. I wait for a carpenter from the village. And how can I hire you for this job? You'll probably ask a too high price from me?"

"This work won't run into money for you," Sergius said, "I need bread, and you have it; I won't demand anything else from you. Don't you know that I work no worse than a carpenter? Why do you need to call another carpenter, old man?"

Then Daniel brought out a dish with mouldy pieces of bread he couldn't eat himself.

"Here, if you want, take everything there is, and do not ask for more."

"Good," the labour-loving hegumen said, "this is more than enough for me; keep it until the ninth hour: I do not take payment in advance."

Having said this, he firmly tightened his belt and got down to work diligently. Till late in the evening, despite hunger, he sawed the boards, hammered in the pales and with God's help he finished the construction, when the sun had already set behind the dense forest. Elder Daniel brought him the mouldy bread again as the agreed payment. The hermit prayed, blessed the bread and started eating it with water, without even salt. Some of the brethren had noticed that while he was eating his bread, earned by the sweat of his brow, the dust of the mould was coming out of his mouth, and, of course, they marvelled at the great patience of their hegumen who did not wish to take even such bad food without working for it. So strictly he observed the precepts of the Apostle: "if any would not work, neither should he eat. (2 Col. 3: 10)"

The brethren however began to grumble at the hegumen because he did not allow them to go to villages to collect alms, and one among them set them all against the hegumen. He said that the hegumen's ban on going to neighbouring villages to collect alms was unfair. The hermits came to Father Sergius and told him they were no longer able to suffer hunger and that the following day they intended to leave the cloister for good. The hegumen addressed the grumbling brethren exhorting them, and while he was still speaking the gatekeeper came running and said that an unknown Christ-loving person had sent plenty of loaves of bread. The first gift was followed by a second, and a third, as abundant as the first one. Manna, angel's bread, had according to the psalmist a special sweet taste for the Israelites. And for his marvellous patience God sent to St. Sergius this wonderful food, for according to David's word "the expectation of the poor shall not perish for ever. (Ps. 9: 17)" Not once, for the sake of the brethren's admonition or simply because of his love for people, was the faith of Father Sergius expressed with such strength as only Christ the Saviour gives to it when He says: "And all things, whatsoever ye shall ask in prayer, believing, ye shall receive. (Mt. 21: 22)"

There was another case, which at first caused grumbling but then turned in favour of God's glory due to the prayers of His servant. When Father Sergius was choosing the secluded place for life in silence, he didn't care about having water nearby. The labour-loving ascetic had been fetching it from afar, in order to tire his flesh even more. It went on this way for seven years after the monastery had been founded. But when more brothers joined the cloister the water shortage became more noticeable. Often the brothers complained about the big distance to the spring. Some of them, the less patient, even rebuked the abbot: "Why have you chosen such a place for the cloister?" Saint Sergius replied to this: "I wished to live here alone in silence; it was God's will to erect a cloister here; keep on praying and do not be despondent. If He brought water out of the rock in the waterless desert for the rebellious Jewish people how could He abandon you, who work for Him day and night in this place?"

Once after admonishing the brethren he went together with a monk to a forest ravine under the monastery. They found some rain water there. The hegumen kneeled and began to pray: "O God, Father of Our Lord Jesus Christ, Thou hast created the Heavens and the earth, both the visible and the invisible, Thou hast created man and Thou dost not have pleasure in the death of the wicked! We, Thy sinful and unworthy servants, plead with Thee, hear us at this hour and show Thy glory! As in the desert Thy mighty right hand performed miracles, drawing water out of the rock, show Thy strength also here, grant us water in this place, and let everyone understand that Thou dost listen to those who fear Thee and glorify Thy name, Father, Son and Holy Spirit, now and ever and unto the ages of ages, amen!"

As soon as he finished his prayer and made the sign of the cross on this place with the rain water, an abundant spring of cold water shot out of the ground and flowed in a fast stream through the valley. Since then the populous monastery has had no lack of water.

Saint Epiphanius testifies that the water was healing and even from afar people asked to obtain this water for the sick.

Father Sergius also allowed laymen to settle in the area around the monastery. That is why after a while the monastery became surrounded by villages and big fields, separated by small woods. One of the busiest roads in Russia, from Moscow to the northern towns, which passed far away from the monastery, was moved nearer to it. After the colonisation of the vicinity of the monastery, a great abundance of everything replaced the initial scarcity, for the settlers zealously provided the monks with all they needed. However the initial isolation of the hermitage and the subsequent remoteness from the inhabited settlements had become a model for the establishment of monasteries in Russia.

Father Sergius, being humble and meek of heart, did not dare to change the monastery's rule. But it was exactly to him that God gave the mission to restore the communal way of life in the monasteries of Northern Russia.

The true, strict monastic life is, first and foremost, a complete renunciation of the world, and subsequently, renouncing all gain and possessions. The Canon prescribes: "Monks should not have any personal possession." Those receiving the monastic consecration are considered as dead to the world: and as the dead possess nothing, so the rule demands that monks should possess nothing. Secondly, the communal monastic life reproduces that very initial community of all the Christians about which the book of the Acts of the Apostles tells: "And the multitude of them that believed were of one heart and of one soul. (Acts. IV: 32)" This is possible only on condition that no one considers anything as "mine" but that they have all things in common. Otherwise conflicts and quarrels amongst the monks are unavoidable as Saints Basil the Great and John Chrysostom say, and no unanimity between men is possible according to Saint Theodore the Studite. Thus, true monasticism should be a strict communal life, about which Saint Theodore the Studite tells his successor as hegumen: "May you guard in every possible way that the brothers would have everything in common, and that nobody would have anything of his own, not even a needle." It doesn't mean that the strict communal monastic rules are the precondition for all true monasticism. This lifestyle is meant for the monastic communities and not for hermits.

In the beginning, when Saint Sergius was first hegumen, when the number of brethren was twelve, there were already transitive customs from secluded life to the communal life in the cloister: common tasks, daily prayers in common. Saint Sergius was inspired by the lives of the great examples of monasticism: Saint Anthony the

Great, St. Euthymius the Great, St. Sabbatios the Sanctified, St. Pachomius the "angelic", St. Theodosius the coenobite. These two last introduced the communal monastic rule: the IVth century Egyptian Saint Pachomius composed the first communal monastic rule; St. Theodosius reformed a number of Palestinian lavras into coenobite (communal) monasteries and created new coenobite ones. The holy lives and the rules of these great ascetics – zealots served as a model for Theodosius of the Caves, who founded in the XIth century the Kievo-Pecherskaia Lavra.

The Mongolian invasion had interrupted the natural course of monastic life: many monasteries had been destroyed together with the cities, many had suffered from massacre and devastation, and not all monasteries of the XIth – XIIIth centuries had been restored later on. The monastic revival began only in the second half of the XIVth century due to the activity of Metropolitan Alexis of Moscow. This coincided with the begin of the overcoming of the Golden Horde's yoke. There is little known about the monasteries in the previous century (second half XIIIth – first half XIVth centuries) but the monastic values had been fully present in the spiritual, moral and social lives. There is no information from original sources about the monasteries and their type at that time, besides the principles of a solitary life, sometimes in combination with certain traits of communal life. The majority of them was located in the cities or on the outskirts and were founded mainly by dukes or boyars (Russian members of the gentry). Such monasteries were meant to be the dukes' or boyar's family burial vaults, the place for their old age; they had more preconditions for a solitary life and the possibility to join them was, probably, limited and conditioned by the size of a contribution. Since the second half of the XIVth century the type of monastic life had been essentially changed. Firstly, a considerable number of new monasteries was established with the coenobitic rule. Secondly, the new monasteries were established in forests or on marshy lands, far away from the cities and barely accessible; more hermitages appeared located far away. And last, thirdly, the founders of the new monasteries were ascetics, like Father Sergius. Such monasteries grew naturally around the hermitages of such hermits, when it was God's will.

The exact date of the conversion of Father Sergius' monastery from eremitical life to coenobitic monasticism is unknown. The change of the monastic rule had been made by the instructions and with the blessing of patriarch Philotheos of Constantinople, whose document was delivered to the monastery by "Greeks" as is written in the chronicles.

Blessed Epiphanius writes that they presented the hegumen with a cross, a paramandia and schema and also a letter in which the patriarch, after he expressed his pleasure at the virtuous life of the ascetic, admonished him to introduce communal life in his monastery. Saint Sergius went to metropolitan Alexis and, having received his blessing, introduced the new monastic rule in his Holy Trinity cloister. This reform made it the first monastery in Russia of a "communal hermitage" type. It probably took place in the second half of the XIVth century. After that a great number of new coenobitic monasteries were established in the course of time.

In general the brethren gladly accepted the new monastic rule. Some were dissatisfied, but they couldn't oppose the will of the patriarch and of the metropolitan. Some of them left the monastery shortly after.

Now hegumen Sergius began zealously to organize the communal life in his cloister. Many new kinds of work and concerns fell on his shoulders. Before, he was mostly asked about spiritual matters: confession of thoughts, sorrows and spiritual needs, while with regard to the material needs every monk took care of it himself. Now he had to take care also of food, clothing and all the necessities of life of the brethren.. The first rule was that every capable monk had to work. The aged and sick had lay brothers to care for them. The hegumen however remained an example of love of labour for everyone.

Father Sergius' Monastery of Holy Trinity

The communal life demanded special premises for meals, bakery, barns, and pantries. And they were all constructed.

The elder brethren were appointed to positions according to the coenobitic rule. The most respectable of the brethren were appointed as cellarers. This duty is known from the foundation of monasticism in Russia: it was established by Saint Theodosius Pechersky. A cellarer in our ancient monasteries carried out the duties of treasurer, housekeeper and sacristan; he was the second in rank after the hegumen and when monasteries had lands, the cellarer managed them, both economically and legally. One of the first cellarers in St. Sergius' monastery was the future Saint Nikon.

Another monk, the most mature in the spiritual life, a humble and meek elder, was appointed as a confessor for all the brethren. Among the first confessors of hegumen Sergius' Monastery was Saint Sabbatius, later on the founder of the Storozhevsky monastery of the Theotokos near the city of Zvenigorod. Later the wise composer of St. Sergius' life Epiphanius the Wise became a confessor.

To keep order and ecclesiastical discipline in church during the Divine Liturgy an ecclesiarch was elected. His duty was to observe the exact execution of the church rules. He had to ask the hegumen's blessing to peal the bells and ministered as senior chorister and partly as sacristan. Simon, one of the closest disciples of hegumen Sergius and future saint, was such an ecclesiarch.

The ecclesiarch had a subordinate, called para-ecclesiarch. He had to maintain the irreproachable cleanliness of the church and to light and extinguish icon lamps, candles, to prepare the censer, and was also in charge of bell pealing according to the ecclesiarch's instruction.

The ecclesiarch had another subordinate, called canonarch, who was in charge of the choir and was responsible for the liturgical books. All the brethren gifted in singing had to sing in the church choir.

As to the church services, the rule of the Stoudion monastery was followed in the beginning as it was simple. But with the establishment of the communal monastic rule in the monastery the Jerusalem rule was introduced since there were enough priests at that time who could perform divine services daily according to the Jerusalem statute, with greater solemnity.

Hegumen Sergius strictly observed the execution of the monastic rules. He required humility and mercifulness from the leaders towards their subordinates, and the brethren were commanded absolute obedience to their superiors. All had to keep a quiet and calm tread, and the head had to be kept bowed so that the appearance would correspond to inner humility. At their moments of leisure the brethren had to stay in their cells and, in order not to be idle, they had to keep themselves busy with needlework or as monks used to say, "minor crafts", because the real work of the monk is prayer and meditating on God for the sake of his soul's salvation. Judging by what remained in the monastery's library and vestry, one of the important cell obediences was the copying of books and the manufacturing of leather for the covers. The monks received clothing and footwear from the monastery. Both the blessed Epiphanius and Saint Joseph Volokolamsky testify that hegumen Sergius sewed clothes and footwear for the brotherhood: therefore it can be concluded that there was a workshop in the cloister. It was forbidden to leave the cloister territory without a good reason. The brethren strictly observed this rule not only during Saint Sergius' lifetime but also after his death.

With the improvement of the cloister, the number of brethren grew even more and there began a time of abundance. In order that this abundance should not lead to negligence or envy and condemnation but instead should multiply blessings, the wise head commanded that his cloister should give shelter to pilgrims. He considered this so important that he even strengthened it by a special promise of God's protection. "If you, my children," so he spoke to the brethren, "will keep my precepts without revolting against them, then even after my death the monastery will prosper and remain for many years by the Grace of Christ."

It seemed that after the coenobitic life was established in Sergius' cloister, the monastery had become strongly protected on all sides against all afflictions, priest-monk Nikon writes, "but who knows, what the coming day will bring? Oh, how earnestly should we watch and pray so that the peace and prosperity won't turn into destruction through the working of the passions hidden in the depth of the human heart!" The arrival of St. Sergius' elder brother Stephen at the monastery caused great sorrow. Stephen probably came with the intention of leading a more strict spiritual life than he did in Moscow. However, with such an aspiration and having given up his rank of hegumen in the monastery of the Theophany he did not give up the passion to hold sway. He was the elder brother of Sergius; they founded the cloister together; maybe he even donated for the improvement of the monastery – all of these things fed his desire to take priority. Stephen's pretensions were probably even supported by some of the monks, who didn't agree with the new rules. Some of them as has already been said, had left the monastery, but also amongst those who had stayed there were, apparently, those who wished to replace the hegumen.

On Saturday Saint Sergius celebrated Vespers and was in the altar, and Stephen stood on the left cliros. Having seen the canonarch holding the book which he had taken with Sergius' blessing, and not his, Stephen asked with irritation: "Who has given this book to you?", and, having received the answer: "The hegumen has given it to me", he shouted: "Who is the hegumen here? Wasn't it me who first set up this place?" And he probably indulged himself in abusing Sergius verbally, for St. Epiphanius finds it embarrassing to quote his further words. Stephen's angry shouting was heard in the altar and in the whole church. The humble hegumen Sergius said nothing. When the Vespers were over and everybody had left the church, Sergius secretly left the cloister.

Metropolitan Philaret of Moscow writes: "The patience, meekness and humility of the Saint are obvious in this act. But one thing is not clear: why did he not make his brother understand, as it was his duty as hegumen? Why, because of just one person did he leave the brethren and the ministry that were given to him by the sacred power?"

And he answers himself: "There are especial ways of saints, the ways which all should revere because they are directed through the special Grace of God and are justified in their consequences. However not everyone has the right to follow such ways because it would be impertinent if everyone would attribute the same Grace to himself." The sagacious Sergius saw that it would be awkward to expose directly on the spot his brother who wanted to be the head of the monastery. In this case unmasking would look like a wrangling about who is the boss. This kind of personal conflict between the hegumen and his assistant (who also had the hegumen's rank), between the two brothers by blood, would be a temptation for all inhabitants of the monastery.

The humble hegumen had gone to his friend, the future Saint Stephen Mahrishchsky, whose monastery was about thirty-seven kilometres to the east of Sergius' cloister (and twelve to fourteen kilometres to the south of Aleksandrov city). Having informed Stephen of his intention to found a new monastery he asked his friend to appoint a monk, familiar with the vicinity. Having searched the impenetrable forests, they chose a place on the bank of the river Kirzhach (which flows into the river Klyazma), ten to twelve kilometres to the south of Mahrishchsky monastery and forty-five to fifty kilometres to the southeast of the Holy Trinity monastery.

The inhabitants of Sergius' cloister were, of course, very much worried by the disappearance of the hegumen. They began to search for him everywhere. At last, Stephen Mahrishchsky told them that their hegumen had gone into a distant wilderness and settled there. Some brethren began one by one to move to Kirzhach. Sergius helped them to build their cells, and then sent envoys to Metropolitan Alexis in order to receive his blessing for a new church foundation. Possibly, the envoys did not tell that the hegumen had abandoned his monastery, but presented the whole case to the metropolitan in a good light. Having received the blessing Sergius immediately started to build the church and to establish the cloister. With the support of neighbouring residents and dukes and boyars he soon erected the church in honour of the Annunciation of the Most Holy Mother of God. Soon after the cloister was organized according to the communal monastic rule.

It is not known whether Stephen tried to become the real hegumen of the Holy Trinity monastery but most of the brethren determinedly desired the return of Sergius. Possibly, after several requests to him directly, which remained in vain, they sent envoys to Metropolitan Alexis, appealing to his power to make their spiritual father return to the monastery. Metropolitan Alexis sent to Saint Sergius two archimandrites with the admonition to comply with the request of the brethren and the promise to remove from the monastery everyone who vexed him. The humble hegumen didn't dare to disobey the metropolitan. He returned to the Holy Trinity monastery. His disciple Roman was appointed head of the monastery on the river Kirzhach. Roman was ordained a priest by the metropolitan.

The holy hegumen was more than fifty years old at that time. He lived for thirty years on the Makovitza. Those seeking silence came from every quarter and gathered under his shelter. Monks leaving their former cloisters considered it more beneficial to live in obedience to hegumen Sergius. Among them were Archimandrite Simon from Smolensk, Sergius' brother, Hegumen Stephen who resigned and continued living in the cloister together with his son Theodore. The great hermit, realizing that it was God's blessing kept praying with even greater zeal and boldness for his beloved brethren.

Once, late in the evening, when he was carrying out his daily monastic rule and was fully immersed in heartfelt prayer for his spiritual children, he suddenly heard a voice which called him by name: "Sergius!" He was very much surprised to hear such an unusual call in the silence of the night; he said a short prayer, opened the window of his cell and was surprised by a marvellous vision: high up in the sky a wonderful light shone and dispersed the darkness of the night, shining brighter than the sun. And an unknown voice spoke to him again: "Sergius! You pray for your spiritual children – the Lord has accepted your prayer.

Vision of Father Sergius

Look around and see, how many monks have gathered under your leadership in the name of the Life-giving Trinity!" He saw a great number of beautiful birds he'd never seen before, they were flying not over the monastery but around its fencing – they were flying and singing and it was unspeakably delightful. And again he heard a mysterious voice from high in the heavens: "So the flock of your disciples will grow in number, and after you they won't become less: they will be blessed with different virtues if only they follow in your footsteps!"

A heavenly joy filled the heart of humble Sergius: the prophetical vision concerned not only him, but all his beloved brethren, all his dear children in the spirit, and he wanted to share the spiritual joy with somebody among his old disciples. The former Archimandrite Simon from Smolensk lived in the cell next to his. Sergius invited him to be the participant of this wonderful vision.

Surprised with the unexpected call of the hegumen in the night, Simon hurried to Sergius' cell, but he was not vouchsafed with the full vision and only saw the wonderful light. Then Sergius told him everything that he had seen and heard, and both of them rejoiced in the Lord with trembling, according to the word of Psalmist.

"Reading this story," wrote priest-monk Nikon (Rozhdestvensky) in 1892, "one will spontaneously look around in the present vicinity of the Monastery: here is Bethany, here is Gethsemane, the Caves, Kynovia, and there, in the thickest of the forest , the secluded hermitage of the Holy Spirit the Comforter; all these monasteries are as children in the full view of their mother – glorious Sergius' Lavra. But let's not forget that these are the younger children, hundred years ago they didn't exist yet; and how many monasteries have been founded within five hundred years by the sons of Sergius' monastery!"

Metropolitan Alexis wanted him to inherit his staff. He had summoned the hegumen to come to Moscow. The aged hegumen went to the metropolitan on foot. "God's servant liked labour until his very old age," remarks the chronicler, "and never rode horses but always went on foot." Metropolitan Alexis received the hegumen lovingly. During the conversation the metropolitan ordered to bring the metropolitan's paramandia with a golden cross embroidered on it and wished to present it to the hegumen. Pretending not to understand the meaning of the gift, Saint Sergius said with a humble bow: "Forgive me, Your Eminence, from my youth I have never worn gold, all the more do I wish to stay in poverty in my old age." Then Metropolitan Alexis declared that he wished to assign to him this paramandia as a token of "the promise of the prelate's rank" and that he wished that Sergius should become the heir of his crozier. Hegumen Sergius was as humble as determined in his refusal. The prelate tried for a long time to convince the hegumen to accept the great dignity, but Sergius said that he would hide in a remote hermitage. Only then did the metropolitan stop insisting and let the hegumen return to his monastery in peace.

Saint Sergius, the great chosen vessel of God, was given by the Lord to the Russian Land in very grievous times, when the Tartars had almost fully occupied it and when internecine strife of the dukes led to bloody battles. Fratricidal wars, Tartar violence, lawlessness, brutal customs of the times threatened the Russian nation with perishing. For more than a century and a half longsuffering Russia languished under a severe Tartar yoke. And, finally, God heard the intercessions of Orthodox Russia - the hour of deliverance was near, and Saint Sergius turned out to be the true defender of the fatherland. According to the historian Basil Kliuchevsky, Saint Sergius buoyed up the sinking spirit of the Russian people, awakened the people's trust in their own power, and inspired them with faith in God's support by the example of his holy life and his high spirituality. By his own way of life, by showing that such a life was possible, Saint Sergius made the grieving people feel that not everything good-natured was extinguished in them: he helped the people to look into their inner darkness and to discern the smouldering sparkles of that very fire, with which their torch-bearer was flaming. "The nation, which for a hundred years used to tremble when only hearing the name "Tartar", had finally plucked up its courage, had risen against the enslavers and had not only found the courage in itself to rise, but also went to search out the Tartar hordes in the steppes and there, it fell upon the enemies like an indestructible wall, and buried them under thousands and thousands of their bones." Whence did the people come from, who had the courage for such an action, of which their grandfathers were even afraid to think? The young duke, the main leader of the Russian joined armies, whom Saint Sergius had blessed for this feat, belongs to the generation which has grown up before the eyes of the hegumen of Radonezh, under his Grace-giving instruction.

Grand Duke Dimitry Ivanovich, when preparing for the campaign, considered it to be his first duty to visit the Monastery of the Life-Giving Trinity to prostrate himself before the Lord and to receive the parting blessing from Hegumen Sergius. He invited his brother Vladimir Andreevich, all the orthodox dukes and army commanders with a selected armed force who were in Moscow at the time, to go with him and after the feast of the Dormition of the Theotokos he left Moscow. The next day they arrived at the monastery. The grand duke told the hegumen: " You already know, Father, what great grief is breaking me, and not only me, but all the orthodox: Khan Mamai has set all the hordes of godless Tartars to move onto the Russian land to ruin holy churches and murder the Christian people. Pray, Father, that God will deliver us from this affliction!"

The holy elder quietened the grand duke with the hope in God, and asked him to attend the Divine Liturgy in the monastery's cathedral. After the Liturgy had been celebrated, the hegumen invited Dimitry Ivanovich, together with the other dukes and commanders to share the monastic meal. The grand duke declined his invitation as he had just received the message from a courier that Mamai was approaching the Russian borders.

Hegumen Sergius however begged him to have the meal in the cloister.

"This meal," he said, "grand duke, will be to the good of you."

The pious duke then consented, and the God-pleaser told him in prophetical spirit: "The Lord God is helping you here; time has not yet come to carry a wreath of victory together with eternal rest for you, but the martyrs' wreaths with eternal memory are prepared now for many of your comrades-in-arms."

Father Sergius ordered to prepare the blessed water and after the end of the meal sprinkled it on the grand duke and all the dukes, commanders and soldiers who were with him. Talking to the grand duke, the holy elder advised him to honour the malicious heathen Mamai with gifts.

"You should, Master Grand Duke," he spoke, "care for and stand up firmly for your subjects, and risk your life for them, and spill your blood, following the example of Christ Himself, Who shed His blood for us. But before that, Master, go to Mamai with truth and humility, for according to your position you should obey the ruler of the Hordes. You see, Basil the Great also pleased the impious emperor Julian with gifts, and the Lord saw Basil's humility and deposed the impious Julian. Scripture teaches us that if such enemies wish to be honoured and glorified by us, we will do this to them; if they want gold and silver, we will also give it to them; but in the name of Christ, for the Orthodox faith we should give our lives and spill our blood. And you, Master, give them the honour, the gold and the silver, and God will not let them conquer us. He will raise you, seeing your humility, and He will destroy their unbending arrogance."

"I have already done it all," the grand duke answered, "but my enemy's arrogance grows even more."

"If so," the God-pleaser said, "the final destruction awaits him, and you, grand duke awaits the help, the favour and the glory from the Lord. We lay our hope onto the Lord and the Most Pure Theotokos that they may not abandon you." And, blessing the holy grand duke who bowed to him, with his holy cross, the God-bearing Sergius said with fervour: "Go, Master, without fear! The Lord will help you to defeat the godless enemies!"

And then, having lowered his voice, he said quietly, so that only the grand duke could hear him: "You will conquer your enemies."

With warm affection the grand duke listened to the prophetic word of the holy hegumen, he shed tears of emotion and asked hegumen Sergius for a special gift for his army, as the blessing and the pledge of the Lord's favour promised to him.

At that time there were working in the cloister of the Life-giving Trinity among the brethren, who struggled under the guidance of Father Sergius against the invisible enemies, two monks: Alexander Peresvet, a former member of the gentry of Bryansk, and Andrew Osliabia, former member of the gentry of Liubetsk. Before becoming monks they both were famous as brave athletes and valiant warriors, very skilled in battle. It was these monks-athletes that the grand duke asked Hegumen Sergius for his army: he hoped that the courage of these two men, people who had entirely devoted themselves to God, would be an example for the troops. The hegumen immediately commanded Peresvet and Osliabia to prepare themselves for battle. The valorous monks joyfully accepted the elder's blessing, and he told them to wear the schema with the image of the Cross instead of helmets and armour. "Here, my children, is the imperishable weapon," hegumen Sergius said, "let it be instead of helmets and shields for you!" Commending them to the grand duke, the saintly elder said to him: "My beloved duke, here are my armour bearers and novices, chosen by you!" He addressed the monks at parting: "Peace unto you, my beloved brethren in Christ! Courage, as valorous soldiers of Christ! The time of your feat has come!" Having blessed with the cross and having once again sprinkled with blessed water the Grand Duke Dimitry Ivanovich, his monks-knights and the entire armed force, hegumen Sergius said to the commander: "The Lord God will be your helper and defender, He will win and will depose your enemies and will glorify you!"

Touched to the depth of his soul by the prophetic speech of the elder, the grand duke answered: "If the Lord and His Holy Mother will send me help against the enemy, I will build a cloister in honour of the Most Holy Theotokos".

Saint Sergius saw the visitors off to the monastery gates and, having given them the blessing for all the orthodox troops, parted with them wishing them all good in prayer.

On his return to Moscow the Grand Duke Dimitry Ivanovich told metropolitan Cyprian about his journey to the Monastery of the Holy-Trinity, about his conversation with the great elder and about his prediction. With cordial sympathy the Metropolitan listened to his story and advised to keep the words of the Hegumen secret until the events would justify the sagacity of the God-pleaser and the Lord would bless his cause with success.

In the meantime, the rumour spread among the Russian dukes that the grand duke had visited the Monastery of the Holy-Trinity and that the duke had received a blessing from the elder Sergius, the hermit of Radonezh, to start battle against Mamai. A small ray of hope flashed in the hearts of the Russian people, and those, who were at one with Mamai, became confused. Such was the Ryazan's Duke Oleg. He was already going to become Mamai's ally to profit at the expense of the Moscow princedom, from which he did not expect a strong resistance, when suddenly he received the news that the huge army under the leadership of the Grand Duke Dimitry Ivanovich had already crossed the River Oka. It meant that he wouldn't be able to unite his army with the army of the Lithuanian Duke Jagail Olgerdovich. He began to reproach his boyars with anger: "Why did you not warn me"? The boyars answered: "We were afraid to tell you though we heard about it long ago. People say that there lives in the lands of the duke of Moscow a zealous monk called Sergius. He has the gift of prophecy from God and he has blessed the Moscow Duke to rise against Mamai". When Oleg heard this, he became very anxious: "Why didn't you tell me about all this before? I would have gone to Mamai then and would have begged him not to go to Moscow this time, and there would be no trouble for anybody then." And the Duke of Ryazan didn't even think of helping the Tartars in their fight against Moscow's army. So the ancient chronicler testifies.

Soon under the leadership of the Grand Duke Dimitry Ivanovich and his brother-associate Vladimir Andreevich, Duke of Serpukhov, the Russian armies reached the Field of Kulikov (in the Tula Region). On September 8th, 1380 from the early morning they were ready to fight standing between the rivers Don and Nepriadva, ready to meet the enemy.

Saint Sergius foresaw the necessity to strengthen the courage of the grand duke once again before the fight and sent him as blessing the Theotokos' prosphora and a letter, the last passage of which has remained in the annals. This message was brought by the monk Nektary, who was accompanied by some brethren. Urging the grand duke to fight courageously for God's holy cause and not to doubt that the Lord would help him to succeed, the elder finished the letter with the following words: "You, Master, should just go [into battle], and God and the Trinity will help you.".

The grand duke read the letter, ate a piece of prosphora and, having lifted up his hands, loudly said a prayer from the Service of the Panaghia: "Great is the Name of the Holy Trinity. Holy Lady Theotokos, help us! By her prayers, my God, and by the prayers of the holy miracle workers Peter and Alexis and the holy hegumen Sergius, help us to fight the opposing forces and save us!"

The message about Saint Sergius' envoy was quickly spread around the regiments. It was as if in their person the great griever for the Russian land had come himself and blessed the troops and this visit was as unexpected as well-timed. Now the weak in spirit were also inspired with courage, and each soldier encouraged by the prayers of the elder, could fearlessly go into battle.

The grand duke bid an honourable farewell to hegumen Sergius' brethren and stood at the top of a high hill. There, beneath him, were the vast ranks of the armies; the breeze fluttered the innumerable banners; in the bright autumn sun the weapons and armours shone. Thinking that many thousands of these brave warriors would fall in the next hours as zealous victims of their love for their fatherland, Dimitry Ivanovich kneeled and, holding out his hands towards the golden image of the Saviour shining in the distance on the black grand-ducal banner, ardently prayed for the last time before the battle...

Then, on his horse, he went round all the regiments, inspiring them and calling the soldiers his "faithful companions and beloved brothers".

"We are ready to give our lives for Christ and our fatherland, and for you, grand duke!" the troops of brave warriors answered from different directions.

Armed with an iron mace, the grand duke stepped forward from the lines of the regiment in order himself to start the battle and to set an example to the others.

"I shall," he spoke, "drink from the same chalice as you. Be it death or life: I'll share it all with you!"

The requests of the Russian dukes and commanders not to endanger himself without need and to spare his costly life for the sake of the common good, could hardly keep him from such a magnanimous impulse. For a while he obeyed their wish and kept for himself only the general command of the battle.

The dreadful moment of the battle which was to decide the fate of Russia, had come; only a small space separated the Russian advanced regiments, where the Grand Duke Dimitry Ivanovich stood, from the innumerable Tartar hordes. In the midday both armies had converged face to face at the Nepriadva creek. Suddenly a huge athlete of a terrible appearance from the Tartar party came forward, his name was Chelibei Tamir Murza; he was a Pecheneg by birth. Vain because of his power, like an ancient Goliath, he shook his spear threateningly and called for one of the Russian warriors to fight in single combat, at the same time abusing the Orthodox hosts. The appearance of this giant was terrifying, and the warriors were thinking: "If only there were one of us who would defeat him!" And though there were numerous brave warriors among them, nobody dared to stand out voluntarily.

Several minutes of languishing waiting had passed, when suddenly there came forward from the regiment of Duke Vladimir one of Sergius' monks: his zealous disciple schemamonk Alexander Peresvet. He addressed the grand duke, dukes and commanders, saying: "Be not confused: our God is great and His strength is great! The proud Tartar doesn't think there's anyone equal to him, but I wish to fight with him. I will fight in the name of the Lord of Hosts! I am ready to receive the wreath of the Kingdom of heaven!"

Instead of armour and helmet Alexander, by order of his hegumen Sergius, wore only the angelic schema. On these clothes, on

the head, the breast and the back there was the sign of the warrior of Christ: the Holy Cross had been embroidered. The valorous
monk-warrior, volunteering for the single combat, sprinkled himself with blessed water, bade in his thoughts farewell to his spiritual
father Saint Sergius, also to his brother-in-arms Andrew Osliabya,
to the grand duke, to all the leaders, orthodox troops and loudly
exclaimed: "Fathers and brethren! Forgive me, sinner!"
"God will forgive you, will bless you with hegumen Sergius' prayers
and will help you!" they answered.
Everybody was moved to tears by the monk's selflessness, and they
all pleaded God to help him, as in ancient times He helped David
fight against Goliath. And Peresvet, dressed in the schema, armed
with a heavy spear, rushed on his quick horse as lightning towards
the terrifying Tartar. Loud exclamations were heard from both par-
ties, the warriors clashed, struck each other with their spears so
heavily, loudly and strongly that it seemed that the whole place of
the fight was shaking and both athletes had fallen dead on the earth!
It was then when the "bloody fight had begun to boil, sharp swords
were sparkling like lightning, spears were cracking," bishop Dimitry
of Rostov narrates, "the blood was flowing, gilt helmets were rolling
under the horses' feet, followed by the heads of the warriors..."
The grand duke did not just stand watching the battle, he dismount-
ed and ordered the commander Michael Brenk to take his horse
and hold the banner. The grand duke put on the clothes of a simple warrior, kissed his pectoral cross with pieces of the Life-giving
Wood, and rushed into battle.
Many valorous Russian heroes found their death during that battle.
The Annals testify that from a hundred and fifty thousand soldiers
no more than forty thousand returned to Moscow. Many commanders had also lost their lives in this bloody battle. But twice as many
Tartars died and it was the total defeat of the hordes of Mamai – the
field was covered with Tartar corpses.

The Kulikovskaya Battle

When the terrible battle of Kulikovo was going on, in the cloister of
the Life-giving Trinity the holy hegumen Sergius had gathered all

the monks together and they had been offering up warm prayers to God for the success of the great undertaking of the Grand Duke Dimitry. With his body Sergius stood in the church of the Holy Trinity, and with his spirit he was in the field of Kulikovo. Seeing everything that was going on there with his spiritual eyes, as if he were an eyewitness, he was telling the monks about the gradual successes of the Russian troops; from time to time he named the fallen heroes by their names; he said the prayers for the repose of their souls and told the monks to do the same. Finally he announced the final defeat of the enemies and glorified God who had helped the Russian warriors.

On his return to Moscow, the Grand Duke Dimitry Ivanovich, who received the name "Donskoy" in honour of this victory, together with his brother and his companion in arms duke Vladimir, who received the nickname "The Braveheart", again arrived at the monastery of the Life-giving Trinity. He wished to express his gratitude to the Lord, to tell Saint Sergius personally about the victory granted by God and to thank him for the warm prayers and for the help rendered by his warriors of the angelic rank. The meeting of the faithful duke with the saintly elder was joyful! Saint Sergius met him at the gates of the monastery with icons and blessed water and, having blessed him with the cross, congratulated him on the victory. The grand duke told the elder the details of the battle, he also told about the feat of the valorous monk Alexander Peresvet, having concluded his speech with the words: "If, Holy Father, your monk Peresvet had not killed the athletic Tartar, many of our warriors would have drank the cup of death from him! But even without him a huge number of the Christian soldiers were killed by Tartars, pray for them, honoured Father"!

"This commemoration is celebrated annually, also nowadays, in all Orthodox Russia under the name of Dimitrievsky Saturday, before the 26th of October (Saint's day of the Grand Duke Dimitry Ivanovich) and it was established, of course, not without the advice of Saint Sergius. Maybe this is the reason why this commemoration is carried out most solemnly in the Holy Trinity Lavra of St. Sergius: the main participants of this battle are commemorated by their names, among them the schemamonks Alexander Peresvet and Andrey Osliabya", priest-monk Nikon (Rozhdestvensky) writes in his book published in 1892.

At that time the valorous heroes had not yet been canonized. Their canonization took place in the XXth century. In 1981 there was established a celebration in honour of the Synaxis of the Saints of Radonezh, currently only venerated locally. These are the Saint the faithful Grand Duke Dimitry Donskoi, Saints Alexander Peresvet and Andrey Osliabya. It is necessary to note that in this synaxis of the Saints of Radonezh, Saint Nektary is also reckoned among them, that very monk who brought the letter of Saint Sergius with the encouraging words for the grand duke and the entire orthodox army to the Nepriadva river.

In 1988 the Saints of Radonezh were canonized as Saints acknowledged in the entire Russian Church. Amongst them there are also dukes Vladimir the Braveheart and Andrew Polotsky, commander Dimitry Bobrok, boyar Michael Brenk.

The grand duke gave generous gifts to the cloister of St. Sergius , and many alms to the people who had gathered from all the neighbouring settlements, he arranged a plentiful meal for hegumen Sergius and his brethren, where he was also present together with all his companions, and he returned to Moscow in good spirits.

Later Grand Duke Dimitry Ivanovich kept his promise: he built the Stromynsky Uspensky cloister near the Dubenka River where the disciple of Saint Sergius, Sabbatius One Eye was the first hegumen. Also on the place of the glorious victory over Mamai on the Field of Kulikovo a monastery was founded in honour of the Nativity of the Theotokos, as the battle took place exactly on the day of this church feast. Now there is a village Monastyrshchina there and a church of the Nativity of the Virgin, which was restored in honour of the 500th anniversary of the Battle of Kulikovo. Simple wooden Royal

Gates, according to the legend given to the church by Saint Sergius himself, have been preserved there as a precious relic.

Documents have been found which testify that it was the "Hegumen of the Russian land" who managed the pacification of the Russian dukes, who were at enmity with the Grand Duke Dimitry. This was of great help to the grand duke, as after the Battle of Kulikovo, his army was very weak. The document, dated 1380, and preserved in the library of the Holy Trinity monastery, testifies that it was the elder Sergius who prevented the assault of the Duke of Ryazan Oleg on the Moscow princedom. The executor of this mission was the cloister cellarer who convinced duke Oleg, and, even to a greater extent, his boyars to abandon the idea of starting an internecine war. After the events of 1380 the Sergius cloister became even more dear to the heart of Grand Duke Dimitry Ivanovich. With the death of Metropolitan Alexis he lost his mentor and entrusted himself with all his heart to the humble hegumen of Radonezh. The duke found in him a wise adviser in matters of state affairs and a warm man of prayer.

He also invited the Elder Sergius to be the godfather of his children Yury and Peter, and he chose hegumen Theodore Simonovsky, the nephew and disciple of Saint Sergius, as his confessor. The brother of the grand duke, Duke Vladimir Andreevich the Braveheart, followed his example and let Elder Sergius baptise his son Ivan. So also did some other dukes and boyars. "A thought," justly remarks Metropolitan, Saint Philaret, "worthy of the men who understand the power of the Christian ascertainment: to choose as godfather an experienced spiritual mentor and a man of prayer."

Those times were troubled and full of anxiety. Reading the chronicles, one finds records saying that such and such duke has gone to the Horde to get himself the title of grand duke. Another has ruined or has appropriated the manor house and the lands of his neighbour; a third has instigated Lithuania or the Tartars to wage war against Moscow. Blood flowed like water during these princely discords and only the wise, imperious word of church hierarchs and such great zealots as Hegumen Sergius, kept the dukes, although not always, from these disastrous and bloody internecine wars .

More than once the hegumen of Radonezh undertook these peacemaking missions. In 1358 during the rule of Grand Duke Ivan Ivanovich, Dimitry's father, hegumen Sergius travelled to Rostov to persuade duke Constantine Vasilevich to accept the authority of the Moscow princedom. In 1363 hegumen Sergius went again to his native city on a "pilgrimage to the Rostov miracle workers". He undertook this pilgrimage, when the grand duke came to know that the Duke of Rostov had received a deed of self-rule from the Horde for his principality. Hegumen Sergius went to Rostov probably not only on a pilgrimage, but also to convince the duke not to undertake hostile actions against the Moscow princedom. As a result duke Constantine Vasilevich promised to be in full dependence of Moscow's Grand Duke.

So, due to the vigilant care and the fatherly guidance of Metropolitan Alexis and to the active participation of Hegumen Sergius of Radonezh gradually the whole Russian land, which was weakened by the discords of the dukes, began to unite under the flag of the Moscow princedom, as the dukes began to understand the necessity of the supreme power of the Grand Duke of Moscow. Also, in people the aspiration to unite awoke, in order to throw off the hated Tartar yoke.

The Holy Fathers distinguish two stages in the spiritual life: the first stage is the narrow way of the cross, full of sorrow, the time of labour, efforts and struggle with oneself and with the enemies of salvation, which are the world and the devil. The second stage is that of the heart resting in God, a deep peace of the soul. The first way is the general one, inevitable for everybody, but the second one is the destiny of the special elects of God's Grace only. Anyway, it is impossible to enter the second stage, without having passed through the first condition.

The Hegumen Sergius accomplished the general way of sorrows and labours of the cross. He was in a continuous struggle, incomprehensible to the world, but inevitable for Christ's disciple. And at last, he won. Passions abated. The world with its temptations did not dare to approach him. "His holy body was clothed in rags," metropolitan Platon writes, "a cramped hut was the witness of his theological meditations, and a simple wooden stick supported his flesh, weakened by works of virtue. But his spirit was full of God's abundant Grace, his heart was fed by those sweets which have the taste of the eternal and imperishable life." The unspeakable light of God's Grace shone quietly in the humble heart of the ascetic.

All of God's gifts were given to him: miracle working, prophesising, consoling and edifying, advising and spiritual reasoning. It was as if there were no material barriers to his spiritual eye, neither in distance nor in time.

The following example of this is known.

Stephen, the Bishop of Perm, was travelling once to Moscow. The road was just twelve kilometres away from the monastery of Hegumen Sergius. The bishop however was in a hurry to meet the newly elected Metropolitan Cyprian and he therefore decided to visit Sergius on his way back to Perm. When his carriage had reached the place where the road to the monastery branched off, the bishop

ordered the carriage to stop. He read aloud "It is truly meet" and bowed in the direction of the monastery with the words: "Let peace be with thee, spiritual brother." Father Sergius was at that moment in the refectory. Having noticed the bishop with his spiritual eyes he stood up from the table, and having prayed shortly, he bowed with the words: "Rejoice also thee, pastor of Christ's flock, and let God's peace be with thee." The brethren were amazed at such an unusual act of the hegumen. Some of them realized that it was caused by a vision and after the meal they asked the hegumen about it. He answered: "At that moment Bishop Stephen, who was on his way to Moscow, stopped at the beginning of the road to our monastery, bowed to the Holy Trinity, and blessed us, humble ones." Some of the brethren, wishing to have confirmation of hegumen Sergius' words, rushed hastily after Bishop Stephen. They heard from his travelling companions that it happened indeed exactly as Sergius said. In memory of the mutual greetings of the holy fathers a wooden cross was erected on the place where Bishop Stephen had bowed and after a while a chapel was built over the cross. Priest-monk Nikon (Rozhdestevnski) writes in his book about a custom in the Monastery of the Holy Trinity which was preserved up till nowadays: "During the meal, before the last course the bell rings, the brethren stand up and the priest-monk on duty says: "By the prayers of Bishop Stephen and Saint Sergius, Lord Jesus Christ, have mercy on us!" After this the brethren sit down and finish the meal."
What attracted people to Hegumen Sergius were the stories about miraculous healings, which occurred owing to God's Grace acting through him. There lived not far from the monastery a pious peasant who had great faith in Sergius. His only son became dangerously ill. The father, full of sorrow and hope, carried his son in his arms to the monastery. "I just have to bring him to God's servant in time," he reasoned, "and he will heal him for sure." When he brought his son into the cell of the Grace giving elder, the boy was still alive. However, while he was asking Hegumen Sergius to heal his son and while Hegumen Sergius was preparing himself for the prayer, the

boy died from a severe fit. The father, having no longer any hope, utterly distressed, began to cry and to reproach Hegumen Sergius that instead of consoling him he made his grief even greater. "What shall I do now?" he cried. "I would be better off if my boy had died at home because in that case I wouldn't be deprived of the faith I had in you, man of God!"

The inconsolable father left the breathless body of his son in the hegumen's cell and went out to make a coffin. God's pleaser took pity on the poor father: when left alone with the dead boy he kneeled and began to pray. He hadn't finished his prayer yet when the child suddenly opened his eyes. Soon the father returned with a chest. The hegumen met him with the words: "It was a mistake of you to revolt in spirit without thoroughly observing the situation first: look, your boy didn't die." The man didn't believe his words, but when the boy looked at him, he prostrated himself at the hegumen's feet, thanking him with many words and exclamations. "You deceive yourself and thank me wrongly," the humble ascetic told him. "When you carried your son to me, he grew exhausted from the severe frost and fainted, while you thought he had died. And then he became warm in my cell and regained consciousness, and again you mistakenly think that he resurrected. So, do not tell anybody that I revived him." The father promised not to tell anybody but was it in his power to hide the joy of a father's heart? The cell assistant and disciple of Hegumen Sergius had noticed this joy and heard the story of what had just happened from the father. And thus this miracle became known to the blessed Epiphanius, who noted it down.

He tells about other miraculous recoveries which took place through the prayers of the Grace giving elder. One of the local peasants became seriously ill and he couldn't eat and sleep for three weeks. His brothers decided to ask Hegumen Sergius for help. "God works so many miracles through the hands of the blessed elder that perhaps He will have mercy also on us," so they reasoned.

And so they brought the sick man to the monastery and having laid him on the ground at the feet of the humble hegumen, they pleaded zealously with him to pray for their feeble brother. Father Sergius besprinkled him with blessed water, pronouncing at the same time a prayer for his healing. Directly the sick man felt relief: he fell in a deep sleep and when he woke up he wanted to eat for the first time in these three weeks. Hegumen Sergius prepared a meal for him and gave him to eat. Feeling perfectly healthy, the man returned home with his brothers.

Another known case of healing was about a possessed nobleman, who was brought to Hegumen Sergius from a distant place somewhere on the Volga river. This man, being tortured by an evil spirit, bit everyone and fought with an inhuman power so that sometimes even ten men couldn't restrain him and he had to be chained. However even the chains were not strong enough for him and he would break them and like the possessed man of Gadarene run to a deserted place and walk there like an animal, until his family would find him and bring him back.

When the rumours about the hermit and the miracle-worker of Radonezh had reached this family, they decided to take the unfortunate nobleman to the man of God. It cost them many efforts to fulfil their good wish: the possessed one opposed this plan with all his might, wailing: "Where on earth are you dragging me? Not only don't I want to see him, I even refuse to hear about Sergius!" He was chained and thus brought to the monastery of the Trinity. When they approached the monastery the possessed one broke the chains in a fit, and, attacking his escort, he shouted: "I can't! I do not want to go in! I want to return to where I came from!" His voice was so terrible that it seemed that he was being torn to pieces from inside and his wild wailing was heard in the monastery.

Hegumen Sergius immediately ordered to sound the bell so that the brethren would gather in the church. The prayer service for the possessed then started and he gradually calmed down and his relatives could bring him inside the monastery walls. Hegumen Sergius went out of the church having the Lord's Cross in his hands and blessed the man with it. The possessed one jumped aside and threw himself into a pool of rain water, shouting awfully: "I am burning, I'm burning in a terrible fire!" And from that very moment he was healed, by Christ's Grace and the prayers of God's servant. His reason returned to him and he quietly answered the question why he had jumped into the pool: "When I was brought to Father Sergius and he blessed me with his cross, I saw huge flames of fire which came out of the cross and seized me. Therefore I threw myself into the pool in order not to be burnt."

The healed nobleman spent several days in the Grace-giving shelter of Father Sergius, praising God's mercy and he returned home in peace.

Once a man, who lived in the neighbourhood of the Monastery of the Holy Trinity became dangerously ill. His brothers, full of sorrow about his lot, brought him to the monastery and pleaded with Father Sergius to heal him. Hegumen Sergius said a prayer and sprinkled the sick one with holy water. Almost instantaneously the sick one felt relieved and fell into a deep and long sleep. When he woke up he felt perfectly healthy again.

The Hegumen of Radonezh was considered by the people to be a comforter of those in affliction, the defender and the helper of paupers. There lived in the neighbourhood of the monastery a man who was a real Shylock. He forced one of his poor neighbours to sell him a hog which the neighbour had been fattening up for his own use, and then he refused to pay the money for his purchase. The offended one went to Hegumen Sergius with his complaint.

Hegumen Sergius invited the offender and turned to him with a fatherly admonition: "My son," he said, "if we believe that there is a God, the Judge of the righteous and the sinful, Father of the orphans and widows, capable to retaliate every sin, so that it is terrifying just to think of His wrath, then why do we not tremble while robbing and doing evil so often, not being content with what He gave us out of His grace? Why do we constantly long for something which is not ours and do we not think of God's patience which once may come to an end? Don't we see with our own eyes that those who do so grow poor, their houses become empty, while an eternal torture is awaiting them in the other world?" Because of these and other words that Father Sergius said, the rich man was so moved that not only he promised to pay for the hog, but to improve his entire life. However when the rich one had returned home, his emotion was gone and not only did he forget his promise to improve his life, but also to pay for the hog he took from his poor neighbour. Next day he entered his larder and saw that the hog's carcass, hanging there, was swarming with worms, though it was winter.

He trembled with fear about the result of his disobedience to the words of the holy elder: he immediately paid his debt. With regard to the carcass which was thrown away, the narrator says that even animals and birds didn't want to eat it, as a kind of unmasking of Shylocks.

Once a Greek bishop from Constantinople had been visiting Moscow. Having heard many stories about Hegumen Sergius, he didn't want to believe them, and kept saying to himself: "How could such a spiritual torch appear in such a land, and even more, in the modern, the *last times*?" He decided to meet Hegumen Sergius personally. However when he was approaching the monastery, fear seized him and when he entered the monastery and saw the ascetic hegumen, he became blind. Then, unwillingly, he confessed to the grace-giving elder his scepticism and, reproaching himself, he asked for the recovery of his sight. The holy hegumen touched his eyes and as if scales fell off them he could see again. From that moment on the Greek hierarch preached everywhere that the Hegumen of Radonezh was an earthly angel and a heavenly man.

God's Grace, however, which abided in the holy soul of the Hegumen of Radonezh manifested itself not only in sagacity or in healing. The disciples of the God-bearing Sergius were sometimes granted to contemplate the elevated state of his spirit in clear images. This was especially so at the holiest moments when he celebrated the

Divine Liturgy, when his soul was as if leaving the visible world and aflame with love for the Lord, and was aspiring to Him with all its being.

When one of the disciples, named Isaac, asked the blessing of hegumen Sergius to practice perfect silence, the hegumen said: "If you, child, wish to keep silence, then tomorrow, after we have accomplished the Divine Liturgy, stay near the Northern Doors, and I will bless you there. The elder wished to bless his disciple after the liturgy, after the communion with Christ's Holy Mysteries when he felt the special working of God's Grace. The reason was that the practice of silence is so elevated and so difficult because of the enemy's temptations that it was necessary to protect the disciple by a special prayer.

Next day Isaac stood at the place that the hegumen had told him. Father Sergius came out of the altar and blessed Isaac by making the sign of the cross with his hand, saying: "Let the Lord fulfil your wish!" At that very moment Isaac saw a wondrous flame of fire which came out of the hand of the hegumen, and felt that it enveloped him.

Thus, protected by the blessing of the hegumen, the disciple began along the path that he had chosen. Even if he would wish to say something quietly, the blessing of Sergius would prevent it. Isaac remained in silence for the rest of his days, according to the word of the Divine Script: "As a deaf man heard not; and I was as a dumb man that openeth not his mouth. (Ps. 38:13)"

Once Father Sergius had been celebrating the liturgy together with his brother Stephen and nephew Theodore, who was ordained a priest by that time. The taciturn Isaac stood in the church. Suddenly he saw in the altar a fourth person, dressed in shining garments, who assisted the three priests. During the Minor Entry this unusual person walked behind Father Sergius, and his face was shining like the sun so that Isaac couldn't even look at him. This appearance opened his mouth and he turned to the reverend elder Macarius who was standing next to him with the question: "What is this wondrous vision, father? Who is this marvellous person?"

Macarius however was astonished himself and answered: "I do not know, child, but I am seized with fear myself. Maybe there came together with the Duke Vladimir one or other priest?"

Duke Vladimir Andreeveitch was at that moment on a visit to the monastery and one of his boyars was attending the liturgy. The monks enquired of him whether there was a priest amongst the duke's retinue. The boyar answered that there was no priest with them. Then the blessed disciples of Sergius realized that it had been an angel who had assisted their Father Superior for "the angels love those who are like themselves."

The liturgy came to an end and the wondrous man became invisible. Both disciples conferred on the vision, and having found a moment, asked Father Sergius about his mysterious assistant. The humble elder first tried to avoid an explanation. "What so marvellous could you have seen, my children? My brother and his son were celebrating the liturgy together with me, and there was no one else with us." The disciples however continued entreating him: "For the Lord's sake, honourable father, do not hide it from us, for we saw the fourth man, an angel-like being, who was assisting you." Then the Elder Sergius told them: "My beloved children! If the Lord God Himself has revealed this secret to you, how can I conceal it? The one you saw was the Lord's angel, indeed: and not only then, but every time, when I celebrate the Liturgy, I, unworthy one, have such a visit. But keep it secret, as long as I live."

The witness of another Grace-giving vision, the blessed Simon, the ecclesiarch, a man of well-tried virtue, saw during the Divine Liturgy, how fire from heaven descended onto the Holy Gifts at the moment of their consecration; how this fire moved along the holy throne illuminating the entire altar, enveloping the holy gifts and surrounding Father Sergius. And when Father Sergius wanted to take the communion, the heavenly, Divine fire curled and entered the holy chalice. Thus God's servant had communicated this fire to himself without being consumed, like the ancient Bush, which was "burning without being consumed".

Simon was terrified by this vision and kept silence, trembling, but it didn't remain a secret for the hegumen that his disciple had been vouchsafed a vision. Having partaken in Christ's Holy Mysteries, hegumen Sergius stepped away from the holy throne and asked Simon: "What was it that terrified your spirit?"

"I saw the Grace of the Holy Spirit, which was acting through you," Simon answered.

"Do not tell anybody about what you saw until the Lord has called me to leave this life," the humble hegumen replied.

Once deep in the night Father Sergius was carrying out his cell prayer rule and singing the Akathistos Hymn before the icon of the Mother of God. Having accomplished the Akathistos, Father Sergius gazed at the icon feeling deep emotion and diligently entreated the Mother of God to look after his monastery. "Most pure Mother of my Christ," the holy elder was appealing, "intercessor and defender, mighty helper of the entire human kind, be also for us, unworthy ones, an intercessor, and entreat incessantly thy Son and our God, so that He will look favourably after this holy place, dedicated forever to the glory of His Name! We call thee, Mother of the sweetest Jesus Christ, to help us, thy servants, for thou hast great motherly boldness towards thy Son and God! Be our saving peace and refuge!" Having finished the prayer, he sat down to have some rest but suddenly his holy soul felt a heavenly appearance approaching and he told his cell assistant, monk Micah: "Be awake, child, we will have a wondrous visit right now." The voice sounded: "See, the Most Pure comes!" The elder stood up and hastily went to the entrance-hall. There he was illuminated by the light which shone brighter than the sun and he saw the Blessed Virgin, accompanied by the apostles Peter, the leader of the apostles, and John the Theologian. Not being able to stand this marvellous radiance and unspeakable glory of the Mother of Light, hegumen Sergius prostrated himself, but the Mother of God touched him with her hand and encouraged him with words of Grace: "Don't be afraid, my chosen one," she said. "I came to visit you because your prayer for your disciples was heard.

Appearance of the Mother of God to Father Sergius

Do not be sad about your monastery: from now on it will have abundance of all it needs and not only during your life, but also after your departure to God. I will never leave this place and I will always protect it." So she said and became invisible.

The elder trembled with fear and joy, for several minutes delight had seized him. When he came to his senses again he saw Micah lying on the floor. The elder could see the Queen of Heaven and hear her voice, but his disciple was struck by terror and only saw the heavenly light.

"Stand up, my child," the elder said quietly. The cell monk stood up, but then he prostrated himself before the elder. "Tell me, father, for the Lord's sake," he asked, "what marvellous vision was that? My soul has nearly parted from my body." However the blessed elder couldn't speak yet because of emotion, his face was shining with heavenly joy. "Wait, child," he said to Micah, "my soul is still trembling from this vision."

When finally the hegumen calmed down, he sent Micah to invite the two most reverend monks of his monastery: Isaac the Taciturn and Simon the ecclesiarch. They came hastily and the hegumen told them about his vision. And all together they held a prayer service in honour of the Theotokos, and Father Sergius spent the rest of the night wide awake, contemplating in his mind the Divine vision, which was the crown on his works of virtue on earth. "Not through divination, not in a dream, but in reality he had seen the Mother of God, as Saint Athanasius the Athonite had seen her," remarks the chronicler.

According to the record in "Nikon's Chronicles" this heavenly visit took place during the fast of the Nativity of Christ, in the night of Friday to Saturday. In memory of this miraculous event a custom was established in the monastery of Saint Sergius to hold every Friday evening, the all-night vigil together with the Akathistos Hymn in honour of the Mother of God in the south-west narthex of the Cathedral of the Trinity. This is the place where according to the legend the cell of Saint Sergius was situated and where now stands beautifully the magnificent icon, which represents this event. "And every Saturday after the early liturgy in the church of Saint Nikon, in the same narthex, the sung service of praise is held in honour of the Mother of God," priest-monk Nikon (Rozhdestvenski) writes in his book.

Half a year before his death Father Sergius was vouchsafed a revelation about the time this would happen. He called all the brethren together and transmitted in the presence of all the office of hegumen to his disciple Nikon, and then he immersed himself in silence. September of the year 1391 came and the elder felt that death was coming nearer.

He again gathered all the brethren around his deathbed and turned to them with his last fatherly admonition. As blessed Epiphanius testifies, Father Sergius commanded his disciples to stick firmly to the Orthodox teaching, to keep like-mindedness with each other, to guard the purity of soul and body and not to be hypocrites, to have sincere love for each other, to beware of evil and impure desires, to be moderate in eating and drinking and most of all to adorn themselves with humility; not to cease receiving strangers, to avoid disputes and to consider the honour and the fame of earthly life as nothing but to await the reward from God.

Thus in his farewell speech the dying elder tried with all the might of his fatherly love to imprint in the hearts, which were faithful to him like children's hearts, the saving rules of the monk's life. He reminded them of many things which he told them before and finally commanded them not to bury him in the church but in the monastery's cemetery with the other departed fathers and brothers. Having noticed the grief of their hearts he comforted them in a voice that was growing faint: "Do not grieve, my children! I go to God Who calls me, and I entrust you to the All-Mighty Lord and His Most Pure Mother: She will be your refuge and the wall against the enemy's arrows!"

Just before the parting of his soul the elder for the last time received the Most Pure Body and Blood of Christ. The disciples held his weakened body: with their help he could raise himself a little in order to meet the Lord, Who came in His Holy Mysteries. Reverentially he partook of Christ's Chalice and sank back onto the death bed.

Filled with the consolation of the Divine Grace, he fastened his eyes on above with tears of joy. "Lord, into thy hands I commend my spirit!" the holy elder said quietly and with this prayer his soul passed away to God, Whom he had loved from the days of his youth. This happened on the 25th September 1391. When Father Sergius breathed his last, an unspeakable fragrance spread in his cell. The face of the deceased righteous man was shining with heavenly bliss, and the brethren around his bed were sobbing.

Several older monks went immediately to Moscow to bring the sorrowful news to Metropolitan Cyprian. They told him about the elder's will to be buried in the monastery's cemetery and about the strong wish of the brethren to bury him in the church of the Holy Trinity that he had built, and asked him for permission. The metropolitan gave his blessing to bury the humble hegumen in the church.

With the sobbing and crying which muffled the singing of the burial service, the monks brought the honourable body of their spiritual father and mentor to the church of the Life-giving Trinity. His burial service attracted a multitude of people from neighbouring and remote villages and cities. Everybody wanted to come closer and to touch the honourable body of the elder or at least his coffin. Everyone was present there: dukes and boyars, respectable elders, hegumens and honourable priests from the capital and a multitude of monks: one with the censer, another one with a candle, yet another with an icon were escorting the holy remains of the blessed elder to his place of rest. He was buried near the right choir.

The body of Hegumen Sergius remained in the ground for 30 years and was then excavated because of a special sign. There lived near the monastery a pious man, who had great faith in God's servant Sergius and therefore he often visited his grave in order to pray there.

Once when he fell asleep after evening prayers at his home, Saint Sergius appeared in his dream and said: "Tell the hegumen of my monastery that it is not good to leave my body covered with soil, while water flows over it." The pious man woke up full of fear and joy. Hastily he went to Hegumen Nikon and told him his dream. Hegumen Nikon decided to excavate the body and told this to the brethren. The news about the digging up of the relics of the ascetic spread far and wide. Many clerics and dukes came, amongst whom the god-child of Saint Sergius: Duke Iuri of Zvenigorod and Galich, one of the sons of Duke Dimitri Donskoy. The chronicles tell that when the relics were excavated, a fragrance spread in the church; the body and the garments of the elder looked as if they were just put there, in spite of the fact, that the coffin was covered with water. The celebration of the opening of the relics took place on 5th July 1422.

The honouring of Sergius as a saint began before the establishment of the formal rules of canonization of a saint. Probably Sergius had become a "national Russian saint by himself, because of being greatly famous." (E. E. Golubinsky, historian of the Russian Orthodox Church). In 1427, just five years after the opening of his relics, there was established in his birth place Varnitsy the Varnitski Monastery of Sergius and the Trinity. His official canonization was announced in the deed of Metropolitan Jonah in the year of 1450, where the metropolitan calls Sergius "Saint" and reckoned him amongst the other saints of Russia.

The monks of the Trinity Monastery believe firmly that their deceased hegumen abides with them in spirit. Once the pious monk Ignatius saw in reality, during the all-night vigil, that Saint Sergius stood in his place of hegumen and sang together with the choir. This vision was the answer of the loving elder from the world behind the curtain to his disciples, the answer to their cordial prayerful crying over his coffin.

Metropolitan Platon, addressing God's servant Sergius writes: "Holy man, who is glorified by us now and always! "He, being made perfect in a short time, fulfilled a long time. (The Wisdom of Solomon, 4:13)" It is now about four hundred years that the Church celebrates your commemoration: but thousands of years will pass and yet your name will remain unforgettable. Even if people would have fallen so low that they would consign your name to oblivion, it will stay eternally with God: it is recorded eternally in the books of life and will never be wiped out. Even if the miracles that you still work would diminish because of God's will, the truth of the Gospel stays for ever and it says: "in this rejoice not, that the spirits are subject unto you; but rather rejoice, because your names are written in heaven. (Lk. 10:20)"

The disciples and associates of the Hegumen of Radonezh established about forty monasteries. From these another fifty monasteries were founded. Thus the spiritual posterity of God's great servant spread all over North-Eastern Russia, everywhere kindling the Grace-giving fire of the spiritual life and pouring out the light of Christian illumination. Here is some brief information about the disciples and spiritual friends of Saint Sergius from the book by priest-monk Nikon (Rozhdeststvenski) with some additions.

1. One of the first monks and disciples of hegumen Sergius was the future Saint Abraham Galitsky, who, in the Meneon is also called Gorodetsky and Chukhlomsky. He passed away on 20th July 1375 at an extreme old age; most probably he was older than his mentor. In Hegumen Sergius' monastery he worked in the bakery, carrying wood and water. After he was ordained a priest he asked Hegumen Sergius' blessing to move to the Galitsky lands. On the mountain near Lake Galitsky the hermit found a miracle working icon of the Mother of God "The Tenderness of Hearts" and built there his own cell and a chapel.

His hermitage became known to the Duke of Galitch Dimitry Fedorovich. Upon the duke's request the hermit brought the found sacred object to Galitch. The holy icon performed many miracles and therefore the duke gave Abraham a donation to build a monastery in honour of the Dormition of the Most Holy Theotokos and persuaded the hermit to become its hegumen. Hegumen Abraham laboured a lot for the sake of bringing the faith in Christ to a wild pagan tribe called Choud. The Mother of God helped him by performing still more miracles through her icon. When the monastery became too populated Abraham left it secretly and established another monastery, in honour of the Placing of the Sash of the Mother of God, at a distance of 90 kilometres from his first monastery. Now the village of Ozerki (Little Lakes) is situated there.

After some time Abraham moved to the river Viga and established there a Monastery in honour of the Synaxis of the Mother of God. In the end he left this monastery and established his fourth monastery, in honour of the Protective Veil of the Most Holy Theotokos, where he passed to his rest in the Lord. "Thus this lamp of humility was brought from one place to another where he has been kindling the lamps of spiritual life."

2. Paul Obnorsky or Komelsky, future saint. A muscovite by origin, he took his monastic vows in a monastery on the river Volga and became later one of the first disciples of the God-bearing Sergius. Similarly to the humble Abraham, in the Monastery of the Holy Trinity he worked in the kitchen and in the refectory. Then he became the cell monk (keleinink) of hegumen Sergius. In this way he laboured for several years. Finally he asked the blessing of hegumen Sergius to retire in solitude in the neighbouring forest. After fifteen years, when the brethren started to visit him he received from the hegumen the blessing to move into an even more remote hermitage. The hegumen at the same time granted a copper cross to his zealous disciple, a lover of silence. After much wandering through the forest Paul found a suitable place for himself in the Komelsky Forest: a hollow in an old lime-tree on the bank of the river Griazovitsa and he lived there for three years in spiritual practices. Then he moved to the river Nourma and made a cell for himself which was just a little bit more spacious than the hollow in which he had lived before. Once the hermit Sergius Nuromsky, also a disciple of the God-bearing Sergius called on him. He saw Paul standing near his cell: flocks of birds were circling around him, some were sitting on his head and shoulders and he was feeding hem. Nearby stood a bear, also waiting for food from the hermit; foxes and hares were running around... This was an image of the life of Adam when he was innocent! When the lovers of silence started to visit him regularly

and asked him whether they could build a cell near him, he rejected them at first. However having remembered the advice of his mentor he asked Metropolitan Photius for a blessing to establish there a communal monastery in the name of the Life-giving Trinity. Because of his deep humility, the hermit Paul was not ordained to the priesthood. Lying on his deathbed at the age of a hundred and twelve years on the 6th January 1429, he told his brethren with tears in his eyes about the burning down of the city of Kostroma by the Tartars many years ago, and on the 10th of January he passed away to the Lord.

3. The future Saint Sergius Nuromsky. This disciple of Saint Sergius of Radonezh lived six kilometres away from the hermitage of Saint Paul Obnorsky. Paul and Sergius were spiritual friends and besides this Sergius was Paul's spiritual mentor. By origin he was a Greek and before joining the monastery of Saint Sergius he was a monk on Mount Athos. Sergius lived and practised works of virtue for a long time in the monastery of Saint Sergius and finally, with the blessing of Saint Sergius, he established the Monastery of the Transfiguration of the Lord on the river Nurma.
Sergius and Paul visited each other regularly and Paul, when Sergius was leaving him, out of respect for Sergius, saw him to the place which was situated approximately two thirds of the way to his hermitage. This place, where the holy friends usually bade farewell to each other, has been marked by a chapel. Saint Sergius Nuromsky passed away on the 7th October 1412.

4. The future Saint Silvestre Obnorsky, who established a Monastery of the Resurrection of Christ twenty-four kilometres away from the monastery of Saint Paul Obnorsky. This servant of God had been leading an ascetic life in the solitude of the forest near the river Obnora, when a lost peasant ran into his cell. After this the lovers of spiritual practices started to settle around him. Metropolitan Alexis gave his blessing to build the Church of the Resurrection of Christ.

The hermit Silvestre often retired to a remote place in the thickest of the forest, which later received the name of "Precious Grove". He came from time to time to talk with visitors. Later a chapel was built on that place. He passed away on 25th April 1379.

5. The future Saint Andronik. Andronik, "quiet, meek and humble", according to the words of the chronicler, was by birth from the Rostov region, where the great Father Sergius came from. The elder loved his disciple for his virtues, complete obedience and prayed for him to God particularly ardently, pleading to protect this innocent soul against the enemy's machinations and to assist him in accomplishing the path of his holy life. Andronik for a long time cherished a wish to establish a communal monastery and he didn't hide this wish from the Elder Sergius.

He chose a place on the outskirts of Moscow, about eight kilometres from the Kremlin on the river Jauza and Saint Sergius came to bless this place. In 1361 the building of the monastery was accomplished. More than once the great elder visited his favourite disciple and gave him support in his spiritual practices. Saint Sergius came there to honour the icon of Christ the Saviour, before his journey to Nizhni-Novgorod in 1356. This icon was brought by Metropolitan Alexis from Constantinople and was granted to the monastery. On bidding farewell, Saint Sergius had a long conversation with hegumen Andronik while they were walking on the road to Vladimir. Later a chapel was erected on the place where they parted.

Andronik trained his successor Sabbatius spiritually, and also future saints and famous icon painters Andrew Rublev and Daniel Cherny, who painted the walls of the Cathedral of the Annunciation in the Moscow Kremlin, the cathedrals of Vladimir and in Saint Sergius' monastery. The icon of the Holy Trinity was painted by Saint Andrew for the Cathedral of the Trinity.

6. Hermit Methodius, future saint. In 1361 he established the Nicolo-Peshnoshsky Monastery. When young he joined the Saint Sergius

monastery and stayed there for several years. With the blessing of Saint Sergius he retired to a thick oak forest near the river Yachroma, not far away from the town of Dmitrov and built his cell on a small mound in the middle of a swamp. When those seeking the ascetic path started to come to him asking for permission to build their cells next to his, Saint Sergius visited them and advised them to build the monastery and the church on another place, out of the swamp.

Methodius personally took part in the building of the monastery, carrying the wood over the river on foot. Therefore his monastery was named "Peshnoshsky", which in Old Slavonic means "carrying on foot", and the river was named "Peshnosha". From time to time Methodius retired to a solitary place two kilometres away from the monastery, where he was visited by Saint Sergius, who instructed him spiritually. This place was nicknamed "Conversation" and later a chapel was erected there.

Methodius passed away eight months after his great teacher, on the 4th June 1392.

Several sacred objects were preserved in his monastery up till the beginning of the 20th century: a small shrine with part of the relics of Saint Sergius of Radonezh; the shrine with the relics of Saint Methodius, his staff and a wooden chalice: the one he had been using for the liturgy. This chalice is now exposed in the museum of Dmitrov.

7. Monk Theodore, future saint, whose worldly name was John. He was a nephew of Saint Sergius, who also admitted him to the monastic vows. John was one of his most diligent disciples. Being ordained he related to Saint Sergius his intention to establish a coenobitic monastery. Saint Sergius gave his blessing to fulfill this plan and personally inspected the place on the high bank of the Moscow river that Theodore had chosen as the place for his monastery. This took place around 1370.

The rumours about the ascetic and zealous life of Theodore attracted many aspirants to his monastery. Grand Duke Dimitry Ivanovich asked him to be his confessor and envoy with regard to church affairs to the Ecumenical Patriarch. Metropolitan Alexis treated Theodore with fatherly love.

Saint Sergius was aware of the great social responsibilities of hegumen Theodore and prayed for him so that his life would flow without obstacles. The great father of Russian monks considered the Simonov Monastery as a relative in Christ to his monastery. When visiting Moscow he would stay in a cell, which was considered to be his personal one. Being a lover of humility and labour Saint Sergius would also till there the ground for the kitchen garden, plant trees and dig together with the other monks the ponds and the wells. There is not far from the monastery a big and deep pond. The legend says that this pond was dug by hand by the first monks of the Simonov Monastery and that Saint Sergius had been working together with them. Therefore this pond is called the "Sergiev Pond". Old inhabitants of Moscow say that many sick people, after having stepped into this pond and praying faithfully for help, were healed. From ancient times every year, on the Feast of Mid-Pentecost, a religious procession comes to the pond to hold the ceremony of the consecration of its water.

Hegumen Theodore later became archbishop of Rostov, where he left a lasting memory of himself: he established there the Convent of the Nativity of the Theotokos.

Hegumen Theodore passed away on 28th November 1394.

8 and 9. From the Simonov Monastery came two zealots of the White Lake, Cyril and Therapont, future saints, who were guided by the admonitions of Saint Sergius. The first one was brought to the Simonov Monastery by Saint Stephen Machrishski, who was a monk in the monastery of Saint Sergius. When Stephen visited the Simonov Monastery he would first of all visit the monk Cyril, who carried out the work of obedience in the bakery. The sagacious

Stephen saw from the beginning what Cyril would become in the future and held affectionate conversations with him on the salvation of the soul. After the passing away of hegumen Theodore, Cyril was for a while hegumen of the Simonov Monastery. However, because of his love of silence, he retired to a solitary cell in the Old Simonov Hermitage. His friend Therapont joined him. After a while they moved together to the Siverskoie Lake near Vologda, in the North of Russia. There Cyril established the coenobitic Monastery of the Dormition of the Most Holy Theotokos in 1397, and Therapont established the monastery of the Nativity of the Theotokos in 1398. In 1408 hegumen Therapont moved to Mozhaisk, upon the wish of Andrey Dmitrievich, the duke of Mozhaisk, and established at a distance of one kilometre from the city the Monastery of Luzhetsk. Saint Therapont passed away in that monastery on 27th May 1426. Saint Cyril passed away on 9th June 1427.

10. About 1373 Duke Vladimir Andreevich, the founder of the town of Serpukhov, conceived a wish to have in his town a monastery, which would be the best teacher of piety. He invited Saint Sergius to advise him. The saintly elder blessed the good intention of the duke and together with him inspected the place of the future monastery. The place had the name "The High Place" as it was situated in the forest on the raised bank of the river Nara, not far away from the river Oka and at a distance of about one kilometre from Serpukhov. On the 2nd December 1373, Saint Sergius started the building of the Church of the Conception of the Mother of God by the righteous Anna. The duke asked Saint Sergius to appoint as hegumen of the future monastery his disciple Athanasius, who accompanied him. Athanasius, a future saint, had joined the monastery of Saint Sergius when young, and Saint Sergius loved him dearly for his obedience and humility. Athanasius didn't want to part from his mentor who in his turn was reluctant to let his disciple go, but the elder said: "This is God's will" and the humble Athanasius obeyed. With the help of the pious duke the building of the monastery was soon

accomplished and hegumen Athanasius gathered many monks around himself.

Saint Sergius often visited his disciple in Serpukhov. He sent the novice Nikon, his future successor, who was the first monk in Athanasius' monastery and later priest-monk. The duke had a church built in the monastery and Metropolitan Cyprian consecrated it. From that time on a close spiritual friendship was established between the metropolitan and hegumen Athanasius. In 1387 hegumen Athanasius moved together with some of his disciples to the Monastery of Saint John the Forerunner in Constantinople. He worked a lot in the field of translation and copying of works of the Holy Fathers and he himself wrote a rule, entitled "The Eye of the Church". From Constantinople he sent many icons to his monastery. Hegumen Athanasius passed to his rest about 1401. His successor in the Vysotski Monastery was his namesake and disciple Athanasius, who after his decease had become famous because of his miracle working. Amongst his other disciples Saint Nikita is known. The monastery of Saint Athanasius preserved a long time some of the garments of Saint Sergius.

11. A year after the founding of the Monastery of Serpukhov, Saint Sergius established a monastery on Kirzhatch. Its first hegumen was Roman, future Saint, who passed to his rest on 29th July 1392.

12 and 13. Leonty, future saint, disciple of the God-bearing Sergius was the first hegumen of the Stromynsky Monastery of the Dormition of the Mother of God on the river Dubenka, which was founded in 1378. Three years later, after the glorious victory on the Kulikovo Field the Grand Duke Dimitry Ivanovich, established another Monastery of the Dormition of the Mother of God on the river Dubenka, which was called "On the island", where the hegumen was Sabbatius One-Eye, also a disciple of Saint Sergius. As the tradition tells the great elder gave to this monastery as his blessing an icon of the Most Holy Theotokos of Cyprus.

14. The future saint, hermit Athanasius, also known as "The Iron Staff", lead an ascetic life on the place where later the Cherepovetski Monastery of the Resurrection was founded.

15. Xenophont Tutansky, future saint, founded the Monastery of the Ascension on the bank of the river Tma, near the village of Tutan, about thirty-two kilometres from the city of Tver. He is commemorated locally on 26th January.

16. Therapont Borovensky, future saint, founder of the Borovensky Monastery of the Dormition of the Mother of God at a distance of about eleven kilometres from the city of Mosalsk (Kaluga Region). According to tradition Saint Sergius blessed him on his leaving the monastery with an icon of the Dormition of the Mother of God. Having walked for a while the zealot became tired and lay down in the shadow of one of the trees. He put the icon on the tree, so that it would protect him. However when he woke up, the icon wasn't there! He started to look for it and found it after a long search in the thickest of the forest, on a pine tree. Therapont considered this as an instruction of the Mother of God that she was favourably disposed towards that place as a place for the monastery and he settled there. Soon other hermits joined him and the monastery came into being. The day and the year of the zealot's demise are not known.

17. Sabbatius Storozhevski, future saint, after the passage of Saint Sergius and the retirement of hegumen Nikon into silence, he became hegumen of the Monastery of the Holy Trinity for six years. In 1398, upon the wish of Duke Yuri Vladimirovich, hegumen Sabbatius founded the Monastery of the Nativity of the Theotokos on the mountain Storozha near the city of Zvenigorod, where he passed to his rest on the 3d December 1406.

18. Jacob Zheleznoborovsky or Galitsky, from a family of gentry Amosov of Galitch by birth. Almost until the very death of Saint Ser-

gius of Radonezh he was a monk in his monastery. Then he settled in the thick forest nearby an iron mine about thirty-two kilometres from Galitch. In 1415 he came to the Moscow Monastery of John the Forerunner near a conifer forest. At that moment the Grand-Duchess Sophia Vitovtovna, the wife of Grand Duke Basil Dimitrievich was suffering a painful delivery. The grand duke sent an envoy to the zealot Jacob asking his prayers and God's servant predicted that Sophia would happily be delivered of the heir to the throne. Sophia indeed gave birth to a boy and the grand duke donated as a sign of gratitude the necessary means for the construction of the monastery of Saint John the Forerunner on the place of Jacob's hermitage. God's servant Jacob passed to his rest on 11th April 1442.

19. Gregory, future saint, the first hegumen of the Golutvinsky Monastery of the Epiphany, founded about 1385. This monastery was built with the donation of the Faithful Grand Duke Dimitry Donskoy in memory of his reconciliation with Duke Oleg of Riazan. It was Saint Sergius whose mediation made this reconciliation possible. The grand duke asked Saint Sergius to choose the place for the monastery and to appoint one of his disciples as hegumen.
According to tradition, when the brethren of this monastery asked Saint Sergius about the place where they could dig a well, he hit the ground with his staff and a spring started flowing. Its water has become famous due to many healings. This monastery preserved for a long time the staff of Saint Sergius which he had with him, when greeting Grand Duke Dimitry Donskoy after his glorious victory.

20. There can be reckoned amongst the disciples of the God-bearing Sergius Pachomius Nerekhtsky, the founder of Sypanov Monastery of the Holy Trinity near the city of Nerekhta in the Kostromskaya Province (passed away on 23rd March 1384), Nikita Kostromsky, the founder of the Kostromsky Monastery of the Epiphany in the city of Kostroma and Nikiphor Borovsky.

The zealots of piety contemporary to Saint Sergius highly appreciated his spiritual experience and valued his wise advice and admonitions. Hence the throng of his holy friends and collocutors. We enumerate some, the most prominent among them.

Dimitry Prilutski, future saint, founder of the Prilutski Monastery of Our Saviour near the city of Vologda. He made the acquaintance of Saint Sergius probably in 1354 when the humble young hermit Sergius came to the city of Pereyaslavl to ask for an hegumen for his monastery. Dimitry was at that time hegumen of the Monastery of Saint Nicolas he had founded on the banks of the Pereyaslavskoe Lake. From that time on he regularly visited Sergius' monastery. In 1371 Saint Dimitry left Pereyaslavl and moved to the lands near the city of Vologda and founded there the in that province first coenobitic Monastery of Christ the Saviour. He passed away to his rest on 11th February 1392.

Stephen Makhrishsky, future saint. The brothers Yourkovsky, who lived near his monastery, afraid that their land would be taken from them and given to the monastery, threatened him with death. His protestations didn't have any effect and he moved away to the river Avnezha, sixty kilometres northerly of the city of Vologda. There he founded, together with his disciple Gregory, the Hermitage of the Holy Trinity. Grand Duke Dimitry Ivanovich donated to the hermitage books and other necessary things but he demanded that Stephen would return to his monastery, which he did. When Saint Sergius once secretly left his monastery because of a temptation, caused by his elder brother's claims to being hegumen, Stephen helped his friend to found a new monastery on the Kirzhach Island. The zealot passed away on 14th July 1406.

Paul and Theodore of Rostov, future saints. When the God-bearing Sergius had visited his native town, Rostov-the-Great, in 1363, these two zealots asked his blessing to build a monastery and to point out a suitable place for this. Having searched in the impassable woods which surrounded Rostov, Saint Sergius had chosen a spot on the bank of the river Ustia and said to the hermits: "God and the Most Holy Mother of God will take care of this place." The hermits founded on this place the Borisoglebsky Monastery. Theodore founded also the Monastery of Saint Nicolas on the river Kovzha which flows into the White Lake. He passed away on 22nd October 1419. Soon after Paul also passed away.

Dionysius, Archbishop of Suzdal, future saint, who took his monastic vows in Kiev, founder of the Pechersky Monastery of the Ascension on the bank of the river Volga at a distance of five kilometres from Nizhni-Novgorod. He passed away on the 15th October 1384 in Kiev.

Euphemius, disciple of Dionysius and future saint, had visited Saint Sergius many times during his stay in Suzdal for the sake of spiritual conversations with him. He founded two monasteries: Vasilievsky Monastery at about five kilometres from the town of Gorokhovets and the Monastery of Christ the Saviour in Suzdal. He passed away on 1st April 1405.

Bishop Stephen of Perm founded three monasteries at the mouths of the rivers Vym, Vychegda and Sysol.

Bishop Michael of Smolensk, the disciple of Saint Theodore of Rostov.

This list is far from complete. It is known for example that on his way back from Nizhni Novgorod Saint Sergius founded the Hermitage of Saint George in Gorokhovetsky Uezd, on the banks of the river Kliazma. The first monks of this monastery were most probably the disciples or the collocutors of the great father of Russian monks, but the records have not been preserved.

It is a known fact that Grand Duke Dimitry Ivanovich Donskoy granted hegumen Sergius a place near his palace in the Kremlin, to build there cells and a church on the occasion of Sergius' stay in Moscow. Later the Monastery of the Theophany was built there, but the name of its founder is not known.

There is a legend in the records of the Monastery of the Holy Trinity in Ryazan that it was founded by hegumen Sergius when he visited Ryazan with the mission of reconciliation of Duke Oleg with the Grand Duke of Moscow Dimitry Donskoy, but it cannot be confirmed by other documents.

Most probably the number of spiritual pupils and friends of the great mentor Sergius, and the number of monasteries that they founded was much higher than what we find in the chronicles, which have survived up till now.

Priest-monk Nikon (Rozhdestvensky) concludes his book with the following inspirational lines: "It was said once to one of God's ancient chosen ones [Abraham], the great father of the believers: "Look now toward heaven, and count the stars if you are able to number them... So shall your descendants be." And to Saint Sergius, the great father of the monks was shown in a vision a multitude of birds and it was said to him: "Look around! Thus the flock of your disciples will multiply!" And this promise of heaven came true: Sergius' fledglings like the birds of paradise flew away all over the East and the North of the Russian Land and glorified God by their wondrous lives; like the stars on the night sky they scattered over their native land and they shine brightly there. And as long as the vain clouds of man's false wisdom doesn't push this wondrous radiance into the background, as long as the spirit of true [spiritual] zeal will blow over Russia, no afflictions will threaten her (Russia) for "the holy seed shall be the substance thereof." (Isaiah 6:13)

* * *

Sources used for the narration:
"Life and Works of our Saint and God-bearing Father Sergius, Hegumen of Radonezh and miracle worker of all Russia." Written by priest-monk Nikon (Rozhdestvensky), future Archbishop of Vologda and Totma. Edition of 2003 of Saint Sergius" Lavra of the Holy Trinity, Sergius Posad.
"Saint Sergius of Radonezh and the Lavra of the Trinity he founded." Academician E. Golubinsky

www.ingramcontent.com/pod-product-compliance
Lightning Source LLC
LaVergne TN
LVHW051454170726
843492LV00002B/682